Sulayman S. Nyang

Islam
in the
United
States
of
America

ABC International Group, Inc

Library of Congress Cataloging-in-Publication Data

Nyang, Sulayman S.
    1. Islam—United States. 2. Muslims—United States.
    I. Nyang, Sulayman S. II. Title
    BP67.U6M87   1999
    297'.0973—dc20   90-44510

    ISBN:1-871031-69-9

Cover Design by Liaquat Ali
Photograph by Ed Grazda by permission.

Published by
ABC International Group, Inc.

Distributed by
KAZI Publications, Inc.
3023 W. Belmont Avenue
Chicago IL 60618
Tel: 7732-267-7001; FAX: 773-267-7002
email: kazibooks@kazi.org/www.kazi.org

To
My late father, Alhaji Sheih Nyang
My fate mother, Fatou Bah
and
My two children
Sulayman Jr. and Edna (Dabba)

CONTENTS

Acknowledgements

This publication is the result of many years of labor and dialogue with friends and colleagues interested in the Muslim experience in the United States of America. A number of people contributed to my understanding of the Muslim experience. Academic colleagues such as Mumtaz Ahmad of Hampton University in Virginia, Akbar Ahmad of the State University of New York at Binghamton, New York, Adib Rashad, Aminah McCloud of Depaul University, Clyde Ahmad Winters and countless others who came into contact with me during my lectures across the country. There are also librarians at Howard University, at the Library of Congress and at the Schomburg in New York who have contributed to my research. Those who deserve special mention here are Mr. Ethelbert Miller, Director of the Afro-American Research Center, Beverly Gray, Director of the Africa and Middle East Section, and her staff at the Library of Congress and Ms. Ayesha Adawiya of the Schomburg in New York.

Another source of support and help to the dissemination of my research efforts are the various Muslim and non-Muslim literary outlets that published over the years some parts of the collected essays in this volume. Versions of many of these chapters have appeared in publications that are no longer in existence. Some of the original outlets for parts of these essays are still in operation and full acknowledgement needs to be made here. The first chapter in this volume appears in the second issue of *American Muslim Quarterly*, a young publication dedicated to the study of Muslims and the American public policy process. The third chapter, which focuses on Islam and the American Dream, originally appeared in the November, 1982 issue of *Arabia*, a London-based magazine that catered to the intellectual needs of British and global Muslim readers. Another version of this same essay appeared in Yvonne Haddad's edited volume on *The Muslims of America* (Oxford

University Press, 1991). Some version of chapter six was serialized in two 1997/8 issues of the *Message International* (New York). The tenth chapter was originally delivered on September 26,1991 as a Keynote presentation to the Indiana Interreligious Commission on Human Equality at a gathering hosted by the Islamic Society of North America in Plainfield, Indiana.

Last but not least on my list of acknowledged persons who contributed to my research efforts and greater understanding of the Muslim presence in the United States of America are the numerous members of the Muslim Student Association chapters, Islamic centers and mosques (*masajid*) who so appreciated my scholarship and community activism that they extended invitations to me to visit their campuses and community centers. Over the last twenty years I have visited hundreds of Muslim communities. Hopefully, many persons from these communities will find this book as a mirror in which they can see themselves. If they see parts of their personal experiences in what I described here below, then I can say to myself that I have communicated the ideas and understandings within the general Muslim community effectively. If I fail to communicate the message from the Muslim grassroots satisfactorily, then I am the only one to blame.

INTRODUCTION

This book is written purposely to give the reader an opportunity to explore the lives and times of Muslims in the United States of America. Working on the assumption that the Islamic experience is here to stay and that Americans will gradually learn to live with and accept Muslim Americans, this author sets out to identify the historical developments that have contributed to the rise and institutionalization of the Islamic faith in the American continent. The work looks at the state of mind of the Muslims and at the conditions which prevailed at the time the article was written. With little or no editorial changes, the original essays are kept very much in the form they appeared in scholarly journals and Muslim magazines. Two justifications are given for this course of action. The first justification for this approach lies in the need to maintain the integrity and relevance of the original article to the readers of the time. Secondly, the articles are not edited to reflect current changes because they are meant to be literary and historical markers for those who are seriously interested in the evolution of Muslim thought and culture in the United States of America.

The collected essays in this volume address many themes that are of interest to readers who wish to know more about Muslims and their religion in the United States of America. The first chapter traces the historical roots of Muslims in the U.S. going back to the claims about a Pre-Colombian Muslim presence in the New World. Although there is controversy over this aspect of the Muslim record, there are some very interesting and stimulating pieces of data that deserve closer attention and study. Sources to these types of materials are referenced and identified for those interested in the earliest times of Muslims in the New World. The second chapter deals with the role of diversity in the development of Islam in the U.S. Here the reader encounters and experiences the multiracial and multicultural dimensions of the Muslim experience. Indeed American Muslims are going through a culture adjustment exer-

cise that can only be compared to the one they face whenever they journey to Arabia to do the hajj rites. There at Mount Arafat the Muslim pil-
grim faces a sea of Muslim brothers and sisters who hail from every
point on the globe and speaking many strange languages. The American
Muslim experiences, especially in the major American cities, are the
closest parallels to the Arafat experience in Arabia. The third chapter
focuses on Islam and the American Dream. This is an essay that tried at
the time of its original publication to show its readers how the American
Muslims were juggling with the demands of pious religious life and the
quest for material and spiritual success in a consumer-oriented society
like the United States of America. The fourth chapter centers on the
development of Muslim institutions. This is an area that deserves
greater attention from research. In this section of the book the author
tries to sketch some trends that are identifiable in this stage of Muslim
development in North America.

The fifth chapter identifies the points of convergence and divergence within the Muslim American community. It examines issues like
identity and discusses in some detail the financial and political challenges facing the Muslim community. It touches on a wide range of
issues that are still about the Muslim discourse on the role and place in
the American society. The sixth chapter looks at the manner in which
the message of Prophet Muhammad is seen in Western intellectual circles. While taking note of the fact that the message of Islam is not palat-
able to many individuals living in the West, the chapter sets out to show
the circumstances and conditions that have conspired to create a civilizational opportunity for peoples of Islamic background to become participants and partners in the American civilization. The seventh chapter
traces the history of the Islamic press in America. Going back to the pio-
neering efforts of Muhammad Alexander Russell Webb, the chapter
shows how the Islamic press evolved over the years and what factors
and forces have been responsible for its growth and development. The
eighth chapter centers on the challenges facing the Muslims in the U.S.
and on what Muslims have tried to do to strengthen themselves and
their communities at a critical juncture in their history in North
America. Chapter nine gives a critical assessment of the media coverage
of Muslims and their religion. Chapter ten is an exploration of the
interfaith dimension of the Muslim presence in the United States of
America. Working on the assumption that Muslim life and culture

would go unknown and unacknowledged by the dominant Christian society if the Muslims fail to express effectively their cosmological construct and their theological understanding of the human condition, this chapter shares with the readers thoughts that the author expressed in an Indiana forum for interfaith and interethnic understanding. The eleventh chapter is an important examination of the question of pluralism in America society from an American Muslim perspective. Many pertinent issues are addressed in this piece and the points of convergence between Muslims and their compatriots of various religious and ideological backgrounds are highlighted in the discussion. The last chapter in the book is a note on an African-American organization whose founding fathers saw it as a vehicle for Islamic propagation in the late 1960's and early 1970's. This movement whose activities still need further discussion and elaboration in the literature on Islam in the United States of America, is yet to be thoroughly researched and documented. Our piece is just a contribution to the study and understanding of a group whose activities are now widely celebrated although many gaps remain in our knowledge of its founders and their membership.

1
ISLAM IN THE UNITED STATES OF AMERICA—AN HISTORICAL PERSPECTIVE

Americans of this century are different from their ancestors in three important respects. They are the beneficiaries of the industrial revolution in numerous ways their ancestors could hardly ever dreamt possible; they are the builders of a new country where multiple identities and cultural and racial diversities are unparalled and unprecedented in human history; they are also the creators and creatures of a multireligious universe where the right to believe differently is not only guaranteed to those wish to believe in anything but to those who wish to believe in nothing. The American Muslim communities scattered around the United States of America are the beneficiaries of this American experience.

The purpose of this essay is to examine the history of Islam in the U.S. and to show the various phases in its evolution and development. Working on the assumption that Islam is here to stay and that the First Amendment of the U.S. Constitution will continue to guarantee equal rights to members of this third branch of the Abrahamic tree of monotheism, this paper contends that Muslims in the U.S. have assimilated in many ways in American society and that the future of this community will depend on the attitudes of the majority community of Christians and the *modus vivendi* of the Muslims and Jews in the country. Another working assumption of this paper is that, though the globalization of the mass media will continue to complicate the problems of co-existence between the Muslims and their neighbors sympathetic to Israel, the Muslim communities would eventually work out a *modus vivendi* with their non-Muslim neighbors through their participation in the American political process and through the emergence and consolidation of a theology of pluralism among the leaders and members of the three Abrahamic faiths in the U. S.

11

A. THE FIRST PHASE IN THE HISTORY OF ISLAM IN THE AMERICAS

In writing the history of Islam in the United States of America one must pay attention to the fragmented data available to those studying and reconstructing this past. This period is ridden with controversy because the evidence is not universally accepted by all parties to the debate. But regardless of how one may feel about the evidence, the fact remains that Muslims or persons believed to be Muslims visited this part of the world in pre-Colombian past.[1] In 1312 Mansa Abu Bakr of Mali is believed to have travelled from the Senegambian region of the African coast to the Gulf of Mexico. This account, which has captured the attention of distinguished scholars such as Basil Davidson of Britain and others in Africa, America and Europe, came to us by way of the writings of al-Omari, a Muslim historian whose work has shed much light on medieval African kingdoms in the sub-Saharan regions of the African continent.[2] This piece of historical evidence received support indirectly from the writings of Leo Wiener, the Harvard University professor who wrote a tome on Africa and the Discovery of America.[3] His book provides data on ethnolinguistic connections between certain peoples of the West African coast and the native Americans living in the Gulf of Mexico region of the Americas. Though Leo Wiener's study was not accorded the much needed attention by his contemporaries, towards the end of the nineteen seventies another scholar by the name of Ivan Van Sertima of Rutgers University in New Jersey was reminding his colleagues in the academy that there were indeed other peoples who came to America before Columbus.[4] His book capturing this argument was the topic of academic debates throughout the United States of America. The timeliness of his book was underscored by the fact that Alex Haley's successful book and television series on Roots had already planted in the popular American imagination that Kunta Kinte was a Muslim slave and that he came from the Senegambian coast.[5] There were two other developments which helped increase the attraction of the Van Sertima book. The first was the greater visibility of American Muslims in American life and culture. The boxing championship of Muhammad Ali and the appropriation of the Malcolm X legacy by young African-American activists associated with the Black Nationalist Movement, together make it easier for Americans of all colors, no matter how skeptical, to give some thought to the possible Muslim discovery of the Americas.[6] The controversy surrounding this aspect of Muslim history in the Americas will continue. Perhaps the archeological findings of colleagues in that area of scholarship would shed some light in the coming years. Until we come across new evidence in this field, we can conclude this phase in the history of Islam by saying that the reality of this period for the moment depends on a narrative passed to our generation by a fourteenth century Arab writer and on a Harvard University Professor's comparative linguistic analysis of African and native American languages.

B. AFRICAN MUSLIMS IN ANTE BELLUM AMERICA

After looking at the first phase in the history of Islam in early America, let us now turn out attention to the period before and after the American Revolution. The writings of Allan Austin have filled many gaps in our knowledge of this period in the history of Muslims in the United States of America.[7] During this period at least ten per cent of the African slaves came from Muslim backgrounds. Some of the Muslim slaves became well known and accounts of their lives and activities have survived to our period. But before we examine more closely this epoch in the history of Muslims and their religion, four points need to be made here. First of all, it should be noted that these African Muslim slaves had different experiences in the Americas. Those who wound up in the Portuguese-and Spanish-dominated regions had a greater latitude in the covert or overt practice of their African religions. Evidence for this claim can be based on the survivals of traditional religious forms in these regions of the Americas.[8] With respect to Islam, the evidence of survival during the period of slavery and after also comes from Brazil and Trinidad, where some of the Muslim slaves successfully returned to Africa and resettled themselves in Dahomey (now called Benin) and Nigeria.[9] The second point is that in North America the harshness of slavery and the determined efforts of the slave masters to separate persons of the same ethnic background made the survival of Islam problematic. To the best of my knowledge, there is no evidence of any African Muslim slave family that survived slavery and maintained Islam as a way of life. This is why I call this period as the sixty years gap between the African Muslim slaves and the African-American Muslims of this century. The third point is that those Muslims who made history and were written about either returned home, as in the case of Ayub ibn Sulayman Diallo (Job ben Solomon),[10] or became freed men and reluctantly converted to Christianity, as in the case of Omar ibn Said of Fayetteville, North Carolina.[11] The fourth point is that during the period of slavery the survivability of Islam among the slaves was an impossibility because the maintenance of one's religion presupposes freedom of thought and practice, a luxury that was incompatible with servitude.

In the remaining portion of this second phase of the history of Muslims in the United States of America, attention will center on details about African Muslim slaves and their experiences in the United States. From the historical record we know that slaves were taken from regions of Africa where Islam had already planted itself. The Senegambia region provided slaves to the southern colonies for several centuries. In both South Carolina and Louisiana, slaves from the Senegambia were widely sought after because of their utility and effectiveness as household labor.[12] Slaves also came from other regions to the south and to the east of the Senegambian rivers. Although not all slaves from the Senegambian region were Muslims, those who were Muslims prior to their capture, tried to hold on to their religion. Muhammadu Sisei of Nianimarou in the upper reaches of the Gambia river and Ayub ibn Sulayman Diallo of Bondu were examples of this saga.[13] Some of these were well known to men like Theodore Dwight, the Secretary of the New York Ethnological Society in the mid-nineteen century, who devoted a significant amount of time and energy collecting materials and documenting the lives and times of Muslim slaves in America. Allan Austin's first book which is a collection of the literary fragments about these Muslim slaves tells us that Ayub ibn Sulayman Diallo came to Annapolis, Maryland where he served as a slave for sometime. This African Fulbe prince was himself an accomplice in the slave trade. However, fate dealt him a bad hand when he was captured by some Mandinka slavers and sold to a British captain. He lived under the yoke of slavery in America for sometime before he was freed later by an English officer of the British Navy and returned to Africa. Douglas Grant described him as the Fortunate Slave. What is striking about Ayub was his knowledge of the Quran and the Arabic language. The sources point to the assistance he gave to scholars who needed his services in translating materials from Arabic to English.

There were other cases and stories about the African Muslim presence in what became the United States of America after the American Revolution of 1776. In addition to Ayub ibn Sulayman Diallo and Omar ibn Said, we have the colorful story of one of the oldest Americans ever to walk this earth, Yarrow Mamouth (Yorro Mahmoud) of Georgetown.[14] This Muslim slave, who is called "Maryland Muslim" in one Smithsonian publication, is immortalized in a portrait by two American artists, one of whom is the celebrated Charles Wilson Peale.

What is striking about the Yarrow story is that he lived to be over one hundred years, that he avoided pork from the butchers of his neighborhood, that he engaged in chanting (doing *dhikr*) while walking the streets of Georgetown, that he became a popular fixture in the daily life of Georgetown, that he saved, lost and then finally saved two hundred dollars to purchase a home at Dent Place in what is now a fashionable district of Georgetown.[15] Accounts from the history of Georgetown say that he was frequently seen swimming in the Potomac and that he used to fire a gun in the air whenever he learned about the birth of a baby in a neighbor's home.[16]

Of these three better known slaves in the U.S. who maintained or tried to maintain their Islamic faith, only two of them made it to Africa. The first one, who is known in the literature as the "Fortunate Slave," went back to his home country of Guinea-Conakry. The second one was Abdur Rahman, another prince who became a slave in Natchez, Mississippi in the United States of America, but was manumitted thanks to the intervention of the Sultan of Morocco. According to the sources of the time, he was able to secure the freedom of his wife but not his children. He reluctantly left the U.S. bound for Guinea by way of Liberia. Unfortunately, he died enroute to his home for reunion after long separation from relatives and friends.[17]

Besides the two slaves who were fortunate enough to secure their freedom and return to their country, there were two others who managed to get their freedom but after old age had already set in. The first one was Omar ibn Said, a slave who fled to Fayetteville, North Carolina and was manumitted by his master many years after his arrival in that town. The second one was Yarrow Mamouth (correctly known as Yoro Mahmoud). Perhaps the oldest American ever to live in these United States of America, according to the records left behind by his contemporaries. As I have shown elsewhere, Yarrow was manumitted by the Bealle family and he spent his remaining days as a free man living in Georgetown.[18]

In writing the history of Muslims in North America, scholars cannot avoid this period. Though no institutions were created by the enslaved Africans and their descendants, the fact remains that some of them tried to maintain an Islamic lifestyle. Two conclusions can therefore be made about this period. The first is that the repressive nature of slavery, especially the peculiar institution of the American South, made it virtually impossible for any form of institutional Islam. The second conclusion is that, though religion is indeed a personal matter for all men and woman, in the final analysis its social dimension makes it imperative for believing individuals to unite with others in maintaining its intergenerational survivability.

C. THE MIGRATION OF MUSLIMS TO AMERICA IN THE NINETEENTH CENTURY

The third phase in the history of Muslim immigration to the United States of America began in the post civil war period when a wave of Arab immigration from the Ottoman Empire began to settle along the eastern seaboard and into the heartland of America in the mid-west. In addition to the Arab Muslims who followed the path already charted by Arab Christians of earlier migrations, there were also immigrants from British India.[19] These Muslim immigrants were also following the familiar path carved out for Indian immigrants by the Sikhs of Punjab. Many of these Indian Muslims joined their Sikh country men in Canada and then moved south to the United States of America. Their journey to the U.S. was by way of the Philippines.[20] Muslim immigrants also came from Southern Europe in countries such as Yugoslavia, Albania and Greece.[21] U. S. immigration records identified Muslims from the Ottoman empire as either Turks or Syrians. The Syrian category was a mixed bag of persons from the area of Shaam (present day Syria) and persons from what is now called Palestine and Lebanon.[22]

Muslim immigrants came also from Central Asia and from what is now called Ukraine in the former Soviet Union. These Ukrainian Muslims from the Ukraine arrived in the late nineteenth century and in the early part of this century. The Muhammadan Society of New York was created by them for the purpose of maintaining their identity in their adopted homeland. Their communities survived up to the late fifties and early sixties.We have accounts of Arabic classes being taught by an Arab student in their place of worship in New York City. These Ukrainians and Muslims from Central Asia, especially in the Turkish-speaking parts of the old Soviet Union, could best be described as "children of the Cold War." Their numbers would increase in time because of the communist invasion and takeover of other areas of the world where Muslims were either in the majority or the minority.[23] Chinese, Afghan, Cambodian and Champa (Vietnamese) and other Southeast Asian groups would soon be added to the list of American Muslims. The list of Muslim immigrants continued to grow as the Cold War created more and more crises around the Muslim world. The postwar revolutions and political upheaval in the Middle East led to an exodus of political refugees from the Arab countries under radical Arab movements such as Bathism and Nasserism.[24]

With the eruption of the Khomeini revolution in Iran in 1979 Iranians came to the United States in droves. Many of these men and women had received education from American institutions of higher education thanks to the large investments in education by the Shah of Iran. In the aftermath of his overthrow many Iranian professionals who felt that life under the Ayatollahs would be "nasty, brutish and short" voted against the revolution by fleeing to the U. S. and Western Europe. Although a significant portion of these Iranians were very secular in their adherence and practice of Islam back home, their second coming to America has led some to rediscover their faith in Islam. To my knowledge there is no sociological study of Muslims, especially Iranian Muslims, which shows the percentage of secular Muslims as opposed to strict adherents.[25] Yvonne Haddad and Loomis have estimated that only ten percent of the Muslim immigrants attend regular mosque services. This is based on a limited sample in their *Islamic Values in the United States of America*.[26] But even if this limited sample can be used as a basis for generation about American immigrant Muslims, the fact still remains that Islam has become more visible in American society than at any time before.

A single thread that links all the waves of Muslim immigrants to the larger tapestry of immigrants descending on American shores is their common quest for success in what has always been believed to be the "Land of Opportunities." Indeed many of these immigrants came here in the hope of striking it rich and then returning home to enjoy their fortune from America. Destiny ruled otherwise, and most of them ended up marrying American brides or ordered a spouse from the familiar surroundings of Mount Lebanon or Syria. It was out of this mixed bag of dreams about America and myths about returning home after making it that combined to lay the moral and psychological foundations of these early groups of immigrants. In retrospect, one can argue that though "the myth of return" still enjoys some support among more recent immigrants, the growing assimilation of most Muslims of the second and third generations has made it more and more imperative for the Muslims to build up structures and develop the mechanisms of self development and self-affirmation.

D. THE DEVELOPMENT OF ISLAMIC STRUCTURES IN AMERICA

The fourth phase in the history of Islam in America and in the attempt to build up Islamic structures and institutions, began with the coming of the Muslim students in the post war period. Attracted to the halls of learning of the American society, and determined to succeed by all legitimate means, many of these young men and women who came here returned home laden with the golden fleece of American higher education. This category of Muslims could also be added to the list of "children of the Cold War." In pursuit of Cold War strategic objectives, leaders of the United States of America created a number of educational programs for the recruitment and training of Third World students. As stated above, many of these young people came and went with diplomas. However, there were others who for a variety of reasons decided to settle down permanently in the U. S. Some of these individuals were the victims of political circumstances in the Muslim world and they decided it was politically prudent to make the U. S. their permanent home. Yet, there were others for whom conjugal entanglements played a far more serious part than anything else in their decision to stay here for good.[27] Regardless of how and why they stayed here, the fact remains that those who embraced the philosophy of the Muslim Student Association (MSA), would later graduate and settle within middle America. Many of these generations of Muslim immigrants graduated from colleges and universities and then became Muslim professionals in the larger society. They are the founding fathers of such Muslim organizations as the Islamic Society of North America (ISNA), the Islamic Circle of North America (ICNA), the Association of Muslim Social Scientists (AMSS), the Association of Muslim Scientists and Engineers (AMSE) and the Islamic Medical Association (IMA). These organizations have created a significant presence among Muslims who are willing to come out of the social and political closet and affirm their faith and their rituals in their workplaces and in those parts of the Public Square where they encounter strangers who are as committed to their faith as those Muslims willing to do missionary work in America's public fora.[28]

In our brief review of the history of the Muslims of the United States of America, we would be in error if we fail to show how the third and the fourth phases have together created the mental and physical spaces for the planting of Islam among the native-born citizens of the country. Since the death of Muhammad Alexander Russell Webb early in this century, the numbers of indigenous Muslims have increased significantly over the last ninety years. This fascination with Islam and the dramatic rise in the total number of Muslims among American citizens, have been traced to conversion and natural birth among the immigrants and the converts.[29] These Muslims who are now seen by society as "converts" would prefer to be called "reverts" instead. The increase in their numbers is largely due to the efforts of Shaykh Daud Faisal, an African-American musician who claimed a Moroccan father and a West Indian mother. Married to another African-American who claimed a Pakistani father and a Grenadian mother, Shaykh Daud and his spouse played a key role in the dissemination of Islam among blacks living in the New York/New Jersey area. Their proselytization efforts (*dawah*) work among the non-Muslims led to the conversion of many members of the African-American community.[30] In addition to the activities of the Shaykh from the State Street Mosque in Brooklyn, New York, there were also the efforts of the Nation of Islam to circulate some understanding of Islamic concepts no matter how distorted they appeared to their Muslim contemporaries in the 1930s. As history would have it, the efforts of the late Elijah Muhammad have done more for the multiplication of Muslim numbers than any missionary work from other groups of Muslims in the country. With the accession of Imam W. D. Mohammed to the top position of the inherited Nation of Islam, dramatic changes began to take place within this powerful black movement.

Imam Mohammed has made history in his successful transformation of the Nation of Islam without any violence or major disturbances among his followers. By focusing on the spiritual elevation of his followers and by urging them to take responsibility for their spiritual growth and development through the institutionalization of autonomy among the heretofore dependent mosques scattered across the U. S., he opened the floodgates of spiritual challenges to his followers and thus enabled them to build individual and collective bridges to the immigrant Muslims at home and the overseas Muslims in the Old World.[32] It is indeed the individual and collective legacies of Shaykh Daud and Honorable Elijah Muhammad that created the intellectual, moral and psychological conditions for other Islamic movements to emerge out of the African-American communities. The Darul Islam Movement, the Islam Brotherhood, Inc., in New York, the Islamic Party of North America headed by Hamid Muzaffrudin, the Hanafi group headed by Abdul Khaalis, and all other smaller and splinter groups were either inspired by Shaykh Daud Faisal or were at one time members of the Nation of Islam.[33]

The history of Islam in the U. S. would be incomplete if we fail to add the role and place of the followers of the Sufi orders in the country. Like the Islamic schools of jurisprudence, the Sufi orders were also brought to the United States of America by the migrating Muslims from the old world. Centered on the mystical dimensions of the Islamic experience and usually quiet about their activities, this aspect of Islam has been most appealing to Americans of European ancestry.[34] Some have suggested that the political quietism among Sufi orders has been one of the reasons for its attraction to this segment of the Muslim community in the U. S. Those who make such statements are usually driven to this conclusion after they have compared and contrasted the manner in which many Blacks, as opposed to most White Muslims in the U. S., have used Islam as an ideological weapon against racial discrimination in the society. Regardless of how one feels about this matter, the fact remains that the White American and the Black American do entertain different reasons for joining the global community of Islam. Such divergent views of American society and such differential attitudes towards the political system and the assimilation of Muslims in the larger society, could easily replicate the divisions within the larger society among the racially diversified membership of the emerging Muslim community. Strategic thinking and planning among the Muslims, one must add, could help obviate this potentially major problem. One group that is trying to build a bridge of brotherhood and sisterhood among the multiracial American Muslim community through its annual Powwow and Quran Intensive Program is the Darul Islam community based in Abiquiu in New Mexico.[35]

But lest we misspeak about the divergent opinions on and the differential attitudes towards American culture among the different Muslim groups, whether Black or White or native-born or immigrant, let it be noted here that the Sufi movement among Muslims is color-blind. Its adherents are drawn from all over the Muslim world.[36] There are advocates from Asia who hailed from areas where the Chistriyya, the Qadriyya, the Naqshbandiyya, the Nimatullahi, and many others located in the Middle East and Central Asia. There are also branches of these orders in Africa where splinter groups have formed over the cen-turies since the arrival of Sufism in this part of the world. In the special case of the United States of America, the Sufi movement has brought elements from almost all parts of Darul Islam. They have in fact taken three different directions. There are those Sufi groups from West Africa, especially the Muridiyya and Tijanniyya orders whose followers from Senegal and the Sahelian region of West Africa have become active ped-dlers and traders in the New York area.[37] Their activities in Manhattan and Harlem have been documented by local New York media. The other trend among the Sufi orders is the attempt to create small communities on the West Coast or along the eastern seaboard of the country. The third trend is the attempt of major Sufi groups like the Naqshbandiyya to mainstream themselves among the non-Sufi Muslim majority in the country. These efforts at planting the seeds of Sufism in American soci-ety and within the traditionally non-Sufi Muslim families have signifi-cant implications for the future of Islam in America. The publishers of the American Muslim Quarterly which seeks to educate Americans and U. S. policy makers about the Muslim community would need to pay attention to the emerging dialogue between the Sufi orders and their fol-lowers on the one hand, and the non-Sufis in the country on the other. Even if there are no dialogues in the old world, the common destiny of the Muslim community in the country has made it categorically clear that such dialogues between Sufis and non-Sufis are necessary.[38]

Another area of life for the Muslim leadership and strategic thinkers is the assimilation of and the extension of goodwill to the Native Americans and the Hispanic Americans who have decided voluntarily to join the ranks of the Islamic community in the U. S. As of this writing, there are hundreds if not thousands of members of these American minority communities who are now counted among American Muslims. In order for the Muslims in the U. S. to make a powerful impression on the larger society, their leadership and the members of the grassroots organizations in various parts of the country must demonstrate the universality of their faith and their serious commitment to break down all barriers that give rise to social and political movements for change in the country.

E. RECENT TRENDS IN ISLAMIC INSTITUTION-BUILDING

After having traced the evolution of Muslim communities in U. S. society, let us now identify some of the recent trends in the institution-building efforts of the American Muslims. Seven trends can be identified for the sake of simplicity and brevity. The first trend is mosque-building. Prior to the 1970's the number of mosques in the United States of America was smaller than what it is today. Three factors have been responsible for this phenomenon. The first is the growing realization of the MSA leadership and the Muslim immigrants that they were not returning to their homelands. Their futures were now in the U. S. and they better start investing in the lives of their children. The best investment, according to this reigning vision, is in the socialization process and in the construction of structures which reinforce and valorize their Islamic identity. The second factor which led to this change of heart and mind among many Muslim immigrants lies in the significant amount of money available to American Muslims for mosque construction. The oil boom in the Middle East created unexpected opportunities for the entire Muslim community, both native-born and immigrant, to take full advantage of this state of affairs. As a result of this boom in the Middle East, American Muslims also witnessed a boom in mosque construction. Evidence for this claim rests entirely on the over one thousand five hundred mosques in the United States of America. The first factor which led to the growing number of mosques is the increase in conversion and in the growing feeling of self-confidence and security among native-born and immigrant Muslims. This psychological feeling is linked to the process of ethnic and regional identity affirmation among the sub-groups within the larger Muslim community in the United States of America. Increasingly, in the urban centers of America, both the native-born and immigrant Muslims are engaged in institution-building. One evidence of a community's physical and social presence within the Muslim community is to secure a piece of the American rock. This metaphorical paradigm for Muslim self-definition and self-affirmation in America is beginning to receive greater attention among observers of the religious scene.

The second trend in the Muslim community in the United States of America is the drive to build Muslim educational centers of learning. Many efforts have been made in recent years. Within the African-American Muslim community, the successors to the late Elijah Mohammed under the leadership of Imam W. D. Mohammed, have renamed the old University of Islam as the Sister Clara Muhammad schools. Dedicated to the memory of the mother of Imam Mohammed, these schools now teach orthodox Islamic values while remaining faithful to a curriculum which prepares its students to navigate the waters of the American marketplace. The academic leaders of this system usually get together to exchange ideas as to how they could improve their teaching methods and raise the quality of education for the young people under their tutelage. In the immigrant Muslim community, the construction of schools is in earnest. Two traditions are beginning to emerge among them. The first is what I would call the Ohio Muslim approach to institution-building. Rather than construct a mosque first and then a school, this community of Muslims built in Dayton a school which has facilities for prescribed prayer (*salat*). This is to say, in the Dayton case, the Muslim parents created a school so that their children can attend an Islamic school Monday through Friday. Their approach to institution-building is premised on the notion that providing education to the young helps guarantee the survivability of the community. The second approach is to build a big mosque in which classes are offered on weekends. This is the general pattern across the country. Its decoupling of school needs from the need for a mosque has led to the reluctant enrollment of Muslim children in public schools.[40]

The third trend in the American Muslim community is the rise of political and social advocacy groups. This growing consciousness about the political system and the role and place of the American Muslims in American political life has captured the attention and imagination of thousands of Muslims across the country. The first Muslim efforts in this direction were those of Abdurahman al-Amoudi and his cohorts who felt that something ought to be done to give American Muslims a place at the political table of brotherhood in America. Like the Black Civil Rights advocates of the fifties and sixties, these Muslims founded the American Muslim Council (AMC) and soon after began to press their claims not against any forms of institutionalized discrimination of Muslims but against any attempts at the political and social marginal-ization of Muslims simply because of their religion. The involvement in voter registration and in the cultivation of politicians by individual Muslims and organizations around the country, clearly testifies to the growing consciousness that, to be recognized, Muslims must go beyond mosque construction to political mobilization and interest articula-tion.[41]

The realization of the danger of social and political marginalization has led to the appearance of another Muslim organization. This second attempt at advocacy for the domestic interest of Muslims is the Council on American-Islamic Relations(CAIR). Born just a few years ago, it too has carved out a niche for itself. Through its chapters and its internet facilities it has created a network of Muslim supporters who monitor local news media for adverse or good reporting on Muslim affairs. Through such networks and calls from American Muslims and recent immigrants who suffered discrimination on the job or elsewhere in American society, it has been quite effective in getting grievances redressed all over the country. Cases involving modestly dressed Muslim women have received attention. Muslims who received sloppy treatment from certain uninformed law-enforcement officers have complained and their grievances examined and addressed by higher authorities. Indeed, CAIR has emerged, in the eyes of some Muslims, as the moral equivalent of the Jewish Defense League of the American Muslims.[42]

In addition to the AMC and CAIR, there are four other groups work-ing on Muslim issues in the universe of American public policy. The list includes the Muslim Public Affairs Council, the American Muslim Caucus, the American Muslim Alliance, and the National Council of Islamic Affairs in New York city. Born originally in Los Angeles, California and now operating a Washington office, the Muslim Public Affairs Council (MPAC) is the brain child of the leaders of the Islamic Society of Southern California. Being perceived to be more liberal than the other Islamic groups save for the Muslim American Society of Imam W. D. Mohammed, this Muslim lobby has made significant strides over the last few years. It has established close ties with the First Lady Hillary Clinton and with officials at the Department of State. Through their efforts and the AMC, the First Lady have hosted two events celebrating the end of the month of fasting of Ramadan (*id al-fitr*) events at the

White House. These events provided Muslim families the opportunity to share the joys of festival (*id*) celebrations with the First Lady and her staff. Although the White House received negative publicity from extremist pro-Israeli supporters such as Steve Emerson, who charged in a Wall Street Journal article that the Clintons were harboring HAMAS sympathizers at the White House, the First Lady apparently was not deterred from hosting the second event, even though this time around the AMC was clearly absent.[43]

The American Muslim Alliance (AMA) is based in Fremont, California and its Executive Director is Dr. Agha Saeed. This organization has been active in California for several years. It is committed to grassroots politics and its leadership is scanning the horizons for greater Muslim political involvement in American life. They are presently playing an important role in the drive to create a national coordinating council. Similar to but somewhat different from the AMA is the American Muslim Caucus based in Dallas, Texas. This body of Muslim politicos have been active in the Lone Star state for sometime and their efforts have been fairly well documented in the local Texas media. Like their Californian counterpart from a major U. S. state, they too are eyeing for a national role and they see the idea of a national coordinating council attractive. Another body of Muslim activists based in the important state of New York is the National Council on Islamic Affairs, founded and kept alive by the recently deceased Dr. Muhammad Mehdi of New York City. This organization bears the personal stamp of the veteran Muslim Arab activist whose most recent effort was to place a Star and a Crescent in the same place where the Christian and Jewish symbols marking the Christmas and Hannukah holidays were located near the White House. Although some of the Muslim groups opposed the idea, the Council in New York went ahead anyway.

Political activism of the predominantly immigrant organizations has been matched in some respect by the efforts at political mobilization among the followers of Imam W. D. Mohammed. Since he took over the old Nation of Islam on February 26, 1975, following the death of his father, Imam Mohammed, has steered his flock away from extremism and along the path of balance and tolerance. His first political act of mobilization in the late seventies was to organize Patriotism Day Parade in Chicago. This parade was designed to assert the American identity of his movement and to restore the faith of his followers in the U. S. and its

institutions. This was clearly a significant departure from the old teachings of his late father. By reversing the old doctrine to make America
acceptable and attractive to his followers, the Imam cleared the way for
some of his followers to enter politics. Several of his followers now
served in various capacities in U. S. local, state and federal agencies.
Charles Bilal, a former Texan mayor, has been one of the best known
both domestically and internationally. A recent addition to the growing
list of American Muslim politicos at the state level is State Representative
Amatullah Yamini of the 23rd district of Onondaga County in the
Syracuse region of New York state. She defeated incumbent Republican
lawmaker Will Morgan with almost two-to-one margin. Successes like
those of Amatullah Yamini have inspired many followers of the Imam
to form the Coalition for Good Government on October 29, 1997 in
Charlotte, North Carolina. The Muslim Journal of January 2, 1998,
described the proposal as a "clearly articulated . . . political vision for
Muslim Americans." The idea has also received the support and
endorsement of political leaders such as Muslim North Carolina state
Senator Larry Shaw. According to a press release published and distributed by the AMA and the AMC, the state representative from North
Carolina has recommended the idea of a National Coordinating
Committee to the leadership of the Coalition for Good Government.

The fourth trend is the opening of permissible (halal) food stores
across the country, especially in major cities of the United States of
America. This trend has created some debates in certain Muslim circles.
Prior to the ubiquity of mosques and halal food stores many a Muslim
adherent to strict diet found the kosher food store as a better alternative
to the non-halal food stores in major cities. However, as a result of the
growing presence of halal food stores in areas with significant Muslim
populations, some of the Muslims are beginning to challenge the tradition of other Muslims who buy kosher food. This trend of development
would eventually call for some ruling from the Muslim jurists in
America. Some jurists in the Middle East and elsewhere have already
ruled that this practice is acceptable if and when there are no halal
stores. The American Muslims who are strict constructionists apparently are not fully convinced and the debate will continue in their circles.

The fifth trend is the proliferation of Muslim publications. There is
no reliable accounting of the number and quality of publications coming from different Muslim groups across the country. Each of the major

national organizations has started its own publications. The most widely read publications among Muslims in the U. S. are the *Message
International* of the Islamic Circle of North America, the *Islamic
Horizons* of the Islamic Society of North America, the *Minaret* of the
Islamic Center of Southern California, and *The Muslim Journal* of the
Ministry of Imam Mohammed in Chicago. Other publications circulat-
ing among the Muslims are *New Trend* of the Jamaat al Muslimoon
headed by Dr. Kaukab Siddiqui, *al-Raya* of the *hizbu tahrir*, the Muslim
magazine of the Naqsbandiyya order based in Mountain View,
California, *al-Jummah* (Friday) of the Islamic Revival Association in
Madison, Wisconsin, *The Orange Crescent* from the Islamic Center of
Orange County, California and The *AMC Report* of the American
Muslim Council. Besides these better known publications, there are
countless regular and irregular publications from local mosques across
the country. Each major mosque publishes a newsletter in which it doc-
uments the activities of its center. There are also women, student and
children magazines. *al-Talib* of the Muslim Student Association of
UCLA and the Sister magazine are two recent additions to the growing
list of Muslim publications.

In addition to print media created ostensibly by Muslims to communicate with one another and to reach the larger society, there are
numerous websites bearing Islamic and Muslim names. Some of these
websites have rich materials for those in search of information about
Islamic history and culture. There are however others whose contents
are polemical and sectarian. This sectarian and ideological tendency
among some of these publications diminishes the chances for dialogue
and meaningful exchange on matters of mutual interest to all Muslims.
Anyone familiar with the vast sources of information in the internet
knows that this behavior is by no means peculiar to the Muslim surfers
of cyberspace since this newly discovered social universe cannot be anything other than a replication of the real world of men and women in
flesh, dancing joyously and feverishly around their shrines of mutual
antagonism and sectarianism.

The sixth trend in the American Muslim community is the drive to
create and maintain institutions of higher learning. The first attempt in
this direction is the establishment of the American Islamic College by
the late Ismail al-Faruqi and his colleagues from various Muslim backgrounds. This effort received the support of the Organization of the

Islamic Conference in Jeddah, Saudi Arabia. Dr. Abdullah al-Nassef of Saudi Arabia served as a key figure in its founding. This college is still in existence, although its record has been mixed in terms of student recruitment and enrollment on the one hand, and faculty recruitment and maintenance on the other. Another institution that has survived and has made some significant progress is the East-West University, founded by Dr. Wasiullah Khan. An entrepreneurial academic leader, this educator from Pakistan has managed to operate a college which has a Muslim founding father, even though its mission and curriculum are not inspired primarily by Islamic considerations. Like the American Islamic College, which started out by offering itself as a hall of learning for prospective Muslim students, the East-West University has over the years evolved into a college for inner city Americans who would like to make something out of themselves under a caring and nurturing environment.

In addition to the two colleges listed above, there are two other efforts at institution-building at the college/university level. The first in terms of historical chronology is the Muslim Teachers College of Virginia. This college is still in an embryonic state. Its founders are committed to the provision of Islamic education primarily to African-American students. The college is located in a rural Virginia where it could grow in time. It publishes a journal called *The Muslim Teacher's College Journal*. Articles cover a wide range of subjects relating to Islamic education. Its moving spirits are Imam Qadir Abdus-Sabur, his wife, Beverly H. Abdus-Sabur, Dr. James H. Rasheed and their colleagues on the Board of Trustees. Though this college enjoys the endorsement of Imam W. D. Mohammed, and its key leaders do identify with the Ministry of Imam Mohammed, it is not an institution of that movement of Islam.

The second recent attempt to build a college/university for the Muslim population in the United States of America is that which is inspired and financed by the International Institute of Islamic Thought in Herndon, Virginia. Conceived several years ago, but realized only within the last two years, the School of Islamic Social Sciences is under the leadership of Dr. Taha Jaber, a learned Muslim jurist of Iraqi background. His institution is literally the new Muslim kid on the block. The leadership of this new institution is banking heavily on the intelligence and goodwill of the large number of highly trained Muslim scholars and intellectuals around the United States who can provide guidance and services to the school. Its objectives are likely to attract persons interested in Islamic Studies. However, the way ahead is fraught with difficulties. In order to situate itself effectively and meaningfully within the American academic landscape, this new institution must have a steady flow of students. It faces the same problems as the other schools discussed above.

F. CONCLUSIONS

In concluding this brief essay on the historical development of Islam in the United States of America, ten conclusions can be made here. The first is that Islam has gone through many developmental changes and is now here to stay. Evidence for this claim is based on the guarantees of the First Amendment and the growing institutionalization of the Islamic faith among both native-born and immigrant Muslims. The second conclusion is that Islam as a culture and a community is becoming a part of the American religious and cultural landscape. Evidence for this is the growing visibility of Muslim names in American media. The American books of names will become increasingly reflective of these new American cultural and religious realities. The third conclusion is that Muslims are becoming more American and more Muslim in their projection of self and group interest. Evidence for this claim rests on the growing success of Muslim advocacy groups such as Council on American-Islamic Relations, the American Muslim Council., Muslim Political Affairs Council, the American Muslim Alliance, the American Muslim Caucus and the National Council on Islamic Affairs. The fourth conclusion is that the proliferation of mosques and schools testifies to the symbolic and substantive presence of American Muslims in the society. Evidence for this claim lies in the fact that today there are over one thousand five hundred mosques and centers across the United States of America. The fifth conclusion of this study is that American Muslims have made progress in securing a niche in the United States of America, but in order for them to be taken more seriously by the political class of this society, they must not only participate in the political process but must also learn to form alliances and coalitions with diverse interest groups in the American society.

The sixth conclusion is that American immigrant Muslims must learn to deal with sectarianism among Muslims in their new home. This attitude and culture of tolerance, which may be absent in the daily life of many immigrants from the old world is already a part of the socialization of the native-born Americans. Although some of the native-born Americans may see and use Islam as fighting ideological weapon in their struggle for social justice in America, the fact still remains that they are fundamentally American in most ways. Evidence for such a claim can be found in the tradition of using Islam among many African-Americans and the political quietism that accompanies such advocates of Islam. The seventh conclusion is that Muslim dietary habits and requirements would gradually sensitize non-Muslim Americans to be more sympathetic to their Muslim neighbors. This will start first at the interpersonal level before it wells to the surface of intercommunal and societal levels.

The eighth conclusion is that American Muslims will continue to face a dilemma in terms of responding to the foreign policy decisions of the United States of America. Because of the diversity of the Muslim community and because the U. S. is engaged in matters affecting Muslim interest in many parts of the Muslim world, there is bound to be occasional distress over U. S. policy options in certain parts of the Muslim world. Evidence for this claim lies in the fact that Muslims from troubled parts of the Muslim world have been very vocal about policies they deem adverse to Muslims in Palestine, Bosnia and Kashmir. The ninth conclusion is that the institution-building efforts of the Muslim would not succeed unless and until the Muslims create both national and local structures that reinforce and support each other. Evidence for this claim is based on the fact that American Muslims have come to the realization that a coordinating committee of all national organizations has to come into being if progress is to be made nationally. The tenth and last conclusion is that American Muslims are vulnerable to both religious and racial prejudice because, though Muslims are drawn from all human colors and nationalities around the world, the American Muslim population has an ethnic mix which does not neatly correspond with the predominantly white population. Evidence for this claim is based on the fact that white racists in America, especially the ones that juxtapose racism and Christianity, tend to see Islam as an Afro-Asian religion, even though Christianity itself has become increasingly a non-European world religion.

Notes to 1
Islam in the United States of America: An Historical Perspective

1 Abdullah Hakim Quick, *Deeper Roots: Muslims in the Americas and the Caribbean From Before Columbus To the Present* (London, England: Ta-Ha Publishers Ltd., 1996), pp.13-37.

2 Basil Davidson, *Lost Cities of Africa* (Boston: Little Brown, 1959), pp. 74-75. This story of an African visit to the New World in pre-Columbian times is based on chapter ten of ibn Fadl Allah al-Omari's *Masalik al-absar fi absar fi mamalik amsar* (Cairo, c.1342 AH). The Arabic original was translated and published in Paris by Gaudefroy-Demombynes in 1927.

3 Leo Wiener, *Africa and the Discovery of America* (Philadelphia: Innes and Sons, 1922).

4 Ivan Van Sertima, *They Came before Columbus* (New York: Random House, 1976).

5 It should be pointed out here that, in addition to his own book on *Roots*, Alex Haley was also the ghost writer for Malcolm X's *Autobiography*.

6 The 1960s and 1970s created a climate of openness among many Americans. The appropriation of Muslim names and West African cultural styles became more and more evident in the activities of those identified with Africa and her past civilizations.

7 Allan Austin, *African Muslims in Antebellum America* (New York: Garland Publishing Inc., 1984).

8 For evidences of the presence of Muslim slave communities in South America and the Caribbean, see Abdullah Hakim Quick, *op. cit.*; Reverend Father Ignace Etienne's two-piece articles published in *Anthropos*, 1909; Gilberto Freyre, *The Master and the Slaves* (New York: Alfred Knopf, 1946 (1971ed.); Carl Campbell, "Jonas Mohammed Bath and the Free Mandingoes of Trinidad: The Question of Repatriation to Africa," Vol.17, No. 2 (Summer,1974).

9 This population of returnees, known as the Brazilians, were not all Muslims. They were not also of mixed parentage only. See J. D. Fage, *A History of Africa* (New York: Routledge, 1988 (1995ed.), pp. 274-75. For more details on the Brazilian Muslim experience, see the following works: Adib Rashad, *Islam, Black Nationalism and Slavery: A Detailed*

History (Beltsville, Maryland: Writers' Inc., 1995), chapters 4-6; Joao Jose Reis, *Slave Rebellion in Brazil: The Muslim Uprisings of 1835 in Bahia*, translated by Arthur Brakel (Baltimore: John Hopkins University Press, 1993).

10 Allan D. Austin, *African Muslims in Antebellum America: Transatlantic Stories and Spiritual Struggles* (New York: Routledge, 1997), chapter 3.

11 Allan D. Austin, *op.cit.*, chapter 7.

12 Allan D. Austin, *African Muslims in Antebellum America A Sourcebook* (New York: Garland Publishing, Inc., 1984), p. 60.

13 Allan D. Austin, *African Muslims in Antebellum America: Transatlantic Stories and Spiritual Struggles* (New York: Routledge, 1997), chapter 3; See also John Washington, "Some Account of Mohammedu Sisei, a Mandingo, of Nyani-Maru in the Gambia," *Journal of the Royal Geographical Society*, VII, (1838), pp.449-54.

14 Allan D. Austin, *African Muslims in Antebellum America. A Sourcebook* (New York: Garland Publishing, Inc., 1984); see also "Yorro Mamout: Maryland Muslim," in Sidney Kaplan, *The Black Presence in the Era of the American Revolution* (New York: Graphic Society, Ltd.,1973), pp.218-219.

15 Allan D. Austin, *op. cit.*, p. 70.

16 This account is reported in the local histories of old Georgetown. For some more details about Yarrow, see my "Islam in North America," in Stewart Sutherland et al., *The World's Religions* (London: Routledge, 1988), pp. 521-22.

17 Terry Alford gives a comprehensive reconstruction of the life and times of Abdurahman. See his *Prince among Slaves: The Story of an African Prince Sold in the American South* (New York: Oxford University Press, 1977).

18 See Nyang, *op.cit.*

19 Abdo A. Elkholy, *The Arab Moslems in the United States: Religion and Assimilation* (New Haven, Connecticut: College and University Press Services, 1966). For extensive bibliographical references to the story of Arab migration to the U. S., see Michael A. Koszegi and J. Gordon Melton, *Islam in North America: A Sourcebook* (New York: Garland Publishing, Inc., 1992), pp. 88-114.

20 Omar Khaliidi, ed. *Indian Muslims in North America* (Watertown, Mass: South Asia Press, 1989); Salim Khan, "Pakistanis in

the Western United States," *Journal of Institute of Muslim Minority Affairs*, Vol. 5, No. 1 (1983-84), pp.36-46; Leona Bargai, *The East Indians and the Pakistanis* (Minneapolis, Minnesota: Lerner Publications Company, 1967); Salahuddin Malik, "Pakistanis" in David Levinson and Melvin Ember, edited, *American Immigrant Cultures Builders of a Nation* (New York: Simon and Schuster Macmillan, 1997), pp.-672-678.

21 George J. Prpic, *South Slavic Immigration in America* (Boston, Mass: Twayne Publishers, 1977), pp.103-105.

22 See Abdo El-Kholy, *op. cit.*

23 The role of the Cold War in the shaping of relations between the West and the Muslim World has been examined to some extent. However, the impact of the Cold War and its unintended policy consequences for Muslim minorities in the West have yet to be studied thoroughly.

24 Abdo El-Kholy points to the rise of Nasserism and Arab Socialism as the reason for the flight of many Arab members of the pre-revolutionary ruling classes.

25 The assumption made about Iranian Muslims is that a disproportionate number would be secular and therefore constitute a sizable portion of the eighty to ninety percent of the unmosqued category of American Muslims. For this claim that the vast majority of American Muslims are unmosqued, see Yvonne Haddad and Adair T. Lummis, *Islamic Values in the United States: A Comparative Study* (New York: Oxford University Press, 1987), p.8.

26 Haddad and Lummis, *op. cit.*

27 Although there are no collected biographies and memoirs written by immigrant Muslims, anecdotal evidence certainly points to many marriages between Muslim students and American women. The vast majority of these marriages have been generally contracted with white Christian women, although Jewish, Afro-American and Mexican women have also been married to these immigrants since the earlier days.

28 I have identified elsewhere and in my lectures around the country, three types of Muslims in the U. S.: (i) grasshoppers: a category consisting of thorough-going assimilationists who are unabashedly secular; (ii) oysters: a group of religious isolationists who prefer to live almost exclusively and intimately within the narrow circle of fellow believers;

(iii) owls: a category whose members try to balance the two extreme positions within their faith community.

29 For some details about Muhammad Alexander Russell Webb, see Emory H. Tunison, "Mohammed Webb: First American Muslim," in *The Arab World*, Vol.1, No. 3 (1945), pp. 13-18. For demographic breakdown of the Muslim community in the 1990s', see Fareed H. Numan, *The Muslim Population in the United States: A Brief Statement* (Washington, D.C.: American Muslim Council, 1992).

30 This account on Shaykh Daud Faisal was given to me and my colleagues from Howard University when we interviewed Sister Khadijah, the wife of Shaykh Daud. The Shaykh had already passed away when we went to Brooklyn, New York for the interview in 1984. For additional materials on his movement, see Aminah Beverly McCloud, *African-American Islam* (New York: Routledge, 1995), pp. 21-24. For evidence of such marriages with members of the fairer sex in Afro-America, see Lurey Khan, daughter of a Pakistani (British Indian subject Fazal Khan who came to America around 1912) in "An American Pursues Her Pakistani Past," *Asia* (March/April, 1980), pp. 34-39.

31 See my Foreword to the book, *Muslims in America Opportunities and Challenges*, edited by Asad Husain, John Woods and Javeed Akhtar (Chicago, Illinois: International Strategy and Policy Institute, 1996), pp.ix-xvii; Kambiz Ghanea Bassiri, *Competing Visions of Islam in the United States: A Study of Los Angeles* (Westport, Connecticut: Greenwood Press, 1997), pp.142-182, especially p.159ff.

32 See Sulayman S. Nyang and Mumtaz Ahmad, "A New Beginning for the Black Muslims," *Arabia:The Islamic World Review*, (July, 1985), pp. 50-51.

33 Nyang's Foreword in Asad Husain *et al., op. cit.*

34 For an introduction to the growing literature on Sufism in the United States, see Michael A. Koszegi's piece on "The Sufi Order in the West: Sufism's Encounter with the New Age," in Michael A. Koszegi and J. Gordon Melton, edited, *Islam in North America* (New York: Garland Publishing, Inc., 1992), pp.211-249.

35 Nyang's Foreword in Asad Husain, *op. cit.*, p. xv.

36 J. Spencer Trimmingham, *Sufi Orders* (London: Oxford University Press, 1971).

37 See my piece on "African Muslims" in David Levinson and Melvin Ember, edited, *American Immigrant Cultures Builders of a*

Nation (New York: Simon and Schuster Macmillan, 1997), pp.20-27; Joel Millman, *The Other Americans How Immigrants Renew Our Country, Our Economy and Our Values* (New York: Viking Press, 1997), especially his chapter 6, entitled "Boubous Over Broadway: The New African Americans.," pp.172-209.

38 See the editorial published in Volume 1, No. 1 of the newly established Muslim magazine of the Naqsbandiyya order published in Mountain View, California.

39 For some illuminating discussion on the connections between some of the Chicanos and the Pakistani community, see Karen Isaksen Leonard's essay on "Punjabi Mexicans" in David Levinson and Melvin Ember's volume on *American Immigrant Cultures,* pp. 723-8.

40 For some discussion on Muslim opinions on education for their younger generations, see Kamal Ali, "Islamic Education in the United States: An Overview of Issues, Problems and Possible Approaches," *The American Journal of Islamic Social Sciences,* 1984, pp.127-132; Aminah Beverly McCloud, *op.cit.,* pp. 118-121; Nimat Hafez Barazangi, "The Education of North American Muslim Parents and Children: Conceptual Change as a Contribution to Islamization of Education," *American Journal of Islamic Social Sciences,* Vol. 7, No.3 (December, 1990), pp.385-402.

41 Steve Johnson, "Political Activity of Muslims in America," in Yvonne Y. Haddad, edited, *The Muslims of America* (New York: Oxford University Press, 1991), pp. 111-124.

42 CAIR's reputation is largely due to its prompt response to cases of Muslim bashing and discrimination. The internet has become one of its greatest ally in educating and mobilizing Muslims across the U.S. and beyond.

43 For Muslim accounts of the recent White House event, see "First Lady Hosts *id* Reception at White House for American Muslims," *Pakistan Links* (Inglewood, California), February 6, 1998, pp. 1 and 32.

44 See the write-up on "Amatullah Yamini Wins Democratic Seat in Syracuse's 23rd District State Legislature," *Muslim Journal,* February 27, 1998, pp.4 and 25.

2
THE ROLE OF DIVERSITY IN THE DEVELOPMENT OF ISLAM IN THE UNITED STATES OF AMERICA

T he Muslim community of North America is comprised of people from all corners of the globe. The community consists of members known as native born, U. S. and Canadian citizens either born into or already practicing Muslim families or converts who decided to join the ranks of the Muslim communities around the continent. The other sector of members are known as immigrants, who initially either entered as students or as emigrating professionals who eventually decided to stay permanently in North America due to political, economic or personal reasons. Living in our mosques and homes are representative samples of the larger Muslim community (*ummah*), from Albania, Afghanistan and Algeria to Yemen, Zambia and Zanzibar the Muslim community as a whole is very diverse. Whether we will develop the understanding and tolerance to appreciate this new phenomenon in world history is something that only history will tell.

In order to examine the historical origins of the present Muslim community and to trace the role of diversity in the formation of a Muslim identity in North American society it is necessary to acknowledge certain limitations. First of all, one must not attempt to impose a definition as to who is a Muslim and who is not a Muslim. This examination is not the product of a theological exercise; rather, it is a sociological analysis seeking to identify the factors and forces which in the last century and a half have identified themselves with some aspects of

Islam as it is known to the scholarly community in the world. Second, an absence of adequate data on the Canadian Muslims limits the study but does not prevent the author from drawing analogies or showing parallels between one region and the other.

EARLY IMMIGRANTS AND THE BEGINNING OF DIVERSITY

In tracing the early beginnings of the Muslim community in this part of the world, five facts should be acknowledged regarding the formation of these communities in North America. First, it should be noted here that the first Muslims who voluntarily emigrated to these shores came from the Mount Lebanon area of what was then known as the Ottoman Empire. Following the footsteps of their Christian neighbors, and determined to succeed in the same manner as these former co-inhabitants of greater Syria, these young men of the Levant were motivated by their quest for financial success in America and driven by a fear of the Ottoman draft system. Not necessarily on a spiritual journey, these young men were hoping to strike it rich quick and go back home resulting in a lack of serious commitment to build any structures reminding them of their Islamic origins. Perhaps it was this lack of established roots that made a prospective Lebanese immigrant to the U.S. change his mind and return to his homeland. According to the story, when an American captain told this Lebanese immigrant that there were no mosques in the U. S., he rethought his decision to emigrate, got off the ship and returned home.

The second fact regarding the formation of the community is that the men from the Middle East came from both the Sunni and Shia communities. Historically competing communities, in North America their sectarian differences did not make one group more committed to Islam than the other and their sociological conditions allowed them both to recognize their predicament and adjust accordingly. Indeed, one can now argue that the principle of tolerance witnessed in North America influenced these Middle Easterners to think differently about sects and group solidarities and created the peaceful co-existence between the Sunni and Shia "Syrians" on the one hand, and the Arab Muslims and Christians on the other.

The third fact that needs to be acknowledged about these Syrians was that they did not build any mosques until after World War I. But to compensate for a lack of physical structures, these men formed small

societies along the eastern seaboard and many of them engaged in peddling, where they could discuss their religion with their American cus-
tomers. Most likely they wore their fez hats, creating not only an impression, but also offering a chance for the curious to probe further about
their lands of origins and the cultural peculiarities of their original
homelands. Two circumstantial evidences from the period lend support
to such speculations. For instance, when David Ben Gurion and another
member of the Zionist Movement landed in New York harbor, they wore
their fez hats. If Zionists had no cultural problem adorning themselves
with the fez, we can also assume that many Arabs from the Ottoman
Empire must have found it culturally self-satisfying to do so as well.
Also, Noble Drew Ali, of the Moorish Science Temple, ordered his male
followers to wear the fez at all times. Perhaps Ali, and the Arab peddlers
of the New York/New Jersey were trying to redefine the identity of their
fellow "Negroes" by insisting on the use of the fez to demarcate their
social and psychological space in American society.

The fourth important point about these Muslims from the Middle
East to remember is that at the time of their immigration into the United
States and Canada, almost all of them came from parts of the Ottoman
Empire. However, during the course of settlement in the U. S. and
Canada, the Arab world split into different national entities. The cre-
ation of Syria, Lebanon, Jordan and Israel changed the nature of the
relationship between the individual citizens of the once unified
Ottoman Empire and created another form of diversity among the
Middle Eastern Muslims. Arab Muslims soon became Lebanese, Syrians,
Palestinians, Yemenis and Iraqis. This splinterization process, which
became a concrete reality owing to the forces of Arab and territorial
nationalism, impacted on the emerging Muslim community in this part
of the world. It is indeed this sense of territorial and national differences
that make some of the political issues in the Middle East sensitive to the
different Muslim communities throughout the country. Although all
Muslim communities are concerned about the Palestinian issue or the
Kashmiri problem, it is indisputable that the Muslims from these two
particular areas of Darul Islam are prone to be more emotionally and
politically active than their co-religionists from other regions of the
Muslim world. Muslim leaders organizing and handling Muslim affairs
must take this diversity into account and realize that it means that
Muslims in the U. S. and Canada are able to live together if they do not

permit old loyalties to compete negatively with their adopted American identity or their global Islamic identity.

Reinforcing some of the points stated above is the history of other Muslim communities that came at the same time or after the Arabs. For instance the South Asian Muslims, originally from Punjab, came to the U. S. in the late nineteenth century and settled along the West Coast of the United States of America. Following in the footsteps of their Sikh neighbors who had already created a reputation of success in the U. S. and Canada, these Muslims entered Canada and the U. .S. by way of the Philippines and worked in farms owned by North American agricultural entrepreneurs.

The success stories of the Punjabis in North America reached British India causing many immigrants to make the journey to the U. S. and Canada in search of the same fortune. Leading to the gradual diversification of the Muslim community, this enlargement of the South Asian Muslim community spanned over several decades, gaining momentum after the Second World War and when the U. S. government sponsored a large number of students from this part of the world to study in the U. S. a large population of these students remained in the U. S. for one of two reasons. Some married American spouses and went on to start families in the U. S. and Canada, while others remained due to the threatening political situations in their homelands. All of these immigrants benefited from the 1964 liberalization of immigration laws in the U. S. and one can argue that the diverse sects, schools of law (*madahib*) and Sufi orders (*taruq*) that exist within the Arab and South Asian Muslim communities reflect the realities of these immigrants.

The same pattern of self-replication exists with the Muslim immigrant communities from Southern Europe. The Bosnian and Albanian Muslims who emigrated to the U. S. early in the twentieth century were also here primarily to reap the benefits of North America; to obtain employment, strike it rich and return home. Among their goals, there was no idea of planting Islam in America. But as time passed, it became evident that their children and grandchildren would remain in North America permanently and for this reason, they saw the need to set up structures for their self-perpetuation and as a result, these Muslims began to adjust to their new realities. One of the first things they learned from their American experience was the logic and ethics of pluralism. Historical evidence tells us that Yugoslavian Muslims, as they were then called, had cordial ties with their Christian neighbors and monies were donated by members of the different religious communities toward the construction of churches and mosques. The Albanian Muslims had similar experiences in the U. S.

Further diversity into the U. S. Muslim community came from the former Soviet Union in Central Asia. Different not only from the other Muslims because of their Soviet background, but also because of their Slavicized names and their bitter experience of persecution under communist rule, these Muslims embraced the American dream and the American way of life and learned to accept differences and work with their Muslim co-religionists to maintain an Islamic way of life. But, like their counterparts in the North American Muslim community, they too brought with them their cultural baggage filled with contents which could act as an obstacle to Muslim unity as a whole as well as greater cohesion among themselves.

HOME GROWN ISLAM AND THE ROOTS OF DIVERSITY

Muslim immigration only presents part of the picture resulting in the overall Muslim diversity in the U. S. and Canada. The other pieces of the Muslim jigsaw puzzle lie in the internal history of America. There are two broad categories of historical actors in this story. White American Muslims, generally female or male spouses of Muslims who embraced Islam, or men and women who in their spiritual journeys found Islam as the answer to their search for the meaning of life, make up the Anglo-Muslim dais (propagators of Islam) who can now trace their history back to the intellectual and *dawah* efforts of Muhammad Alexander Russell Webb. Sufi orders such as the Nimatullah, the Qadriyya, the M. T. O., the Bawa group, and the Mariamiyya have historically attracted many whites due to the fact that Sufi orders thrive among those who are more intellectual and mystical in their understanding of and attitude toward Islam. Though Sufism has been a major factor for many of these people, one cannot stereotypically identify all or even most whites with Sufi orders.

The second historical strand in the history of Muslim diversity is the African-American one, which can now be traced back to the efforts of early converts to Islam. Although an undetermined number of African-Americans gravitated to Islam at the beginning of this century, not much is known about them. Evidence about their existence comes through references made by foreign Muslim missionaries such as those from the Ahmadiyyat Islam, an originally Islamic reform group founded in British India by Mirza Ghulam Ahmad in the late nineteenth century.

There are many prominent African-Americans whose activities influenced the course of Islam in the U. S., such as Shaykh Dawud Faisal of the Islamic Mission of the United States of America, the Honorable Elijah Muhammad of the Nation of Islam (NOI) and El-Hajj Malik Shabbaz, also of the Nation of Islam and later, the African-American Mosque, Inc.

These African-American Muslims left behind a mixed legacy of distinct characteristics that brought about an increased diversity among the Muslims in America. These manifestations of diversity became evident in 1975, when Imam W. D. Muhammad succeeded his father, the late Honorable Elijah Muhammad. This legacy of diversity amongst the African-American Muslims did not come easy. To begin with there was a history of confrontation and opposition to the anti-racist racism of the old Nation of Islam which developed among Sunni Muslims in Afro-America. Vigorously opposed to the deification of NOI founder W. D. Farad Muhammad, and to the prophethood of long-time NOI leader the Honorable Elijah Muhammad, the Darul Islam movement, the Islamic Party of North America, the Islamic Brotherhood, Inc. of New York and the Hanafi Movement in Washington, D.C., continually found themselves back in combat against the Nation of Islam.

The death of the Honorable Elijah Muhammad increased the diversity by resulting in a splinterization process within the Afro-American Muslim community. The contest for leadership within the NOI was intense, with each contender rationalizing and justifying their claims through statements of the late Honorable Elijah Muhammad in order to justify the need to establish their own organizations. From these arguments emerged four organizations out of the old NOI: (1.) the reconstructed NOI under the leadership of Imam W. D. Muhammad; (2.) the NOI under Minister Louis Farrakhan; (3.) the NOI under John Muhammad, a brother of Elijah Muhammad; (4.) the NOI under the leadership of Silas Muhammad.

In the late 1970s, African American Muslims began to witness the acceptance of Shia and Sufi teaching among their ranks. Those embracing Shiism were, in many instances, attracted to the messages of the Iranian Revolution of 1979 and some of them even ventured to go to

Iran to complete their higher education. Another group of African-Americans, not a sizable number but significant enough to attract scholarly attention, were attracted by Sufi teachings. These Sufi groups that attract African-Americans are usually African in origins. For instance, the Tijaniyya and Muridiyya groups of Senegal have made some inroads. Mainly found in the eastern seaboard, particularly in New York City where Senegalese immigrants are heavily involved in petty trade and peddling in Harlem, these Sufi groups also have centers in Washington, D. C. and Atlanta, Georgia. Due to their diverse memberships and compositions the Sufi groups bring into the larger Muslim community a different pattern of organization and leadership.

In summary, the emigration of Muslims to the U. S. during the last century, and the home-grown development of Islam in this century among native Americans such as Muhammad Alexander Russell Webb and Shaykh Dawud Faisal, have together led to the emergence of two main categories of Muslims: the native-born and the immigrants. As well as the transformation of the NOI has given rise to new forms of self-definition and hence the greater diversification of the Muslim community. And finally the acceptance of Shia and Sufi beliefs among American Muslims has also added to the diversity among the Muslim population in the United States of America.

DIVERSITY AND DIFFERENT PATTERNS OF LEADERSHIP

The nature of leadership among the Muslims in the U. S. is reflective of the different groups identified above. Based on the evidence available from the different Muslim groups living in the U. S., one can identify five models of leadership.

The first model of leadership is the Amir type of leader. Under this arrangement, a Muslim community finds its mosque dominated by a charismatic leader who is not restrained by any rational, legal mechanism of control. The Amir does only leads prayers in the mosque, but he also exercises control over all affairs of the community. Under this type of leadership power resides in one place and interpretations of Islamic issues lie within the Amir's domain.

The second model of leadership is the board of directors type. This corporate model is adopted mainly by immigrant Muslims who wish to run their affairs very much like the American associations. In this situation, the board members, not necessarily elected by the members of their mosque, are usually governed by a constitution. This model is found either in mosques where board members are elected for time specified terms or in Islamic centers, built by the efforts of founding fathers who have constituted themselves into a board of directors.

The third model of community leadership is the satellite mosque where leadership resides in the hands of a local leader of a community of believers who are more broadly identified with a national or international Muslim group. Such a model incorporates two elements; the idea of elected leadership through the application of the Islamic principle of consultation (*shura*), and the idea of an "imported Imam." In a satellite mosque situation, the Imam is a part of a group of leaders locally accountable to the members of their community mosque and nationally or internationally to the leaders of their base organization.

The fourth model is the independent local mosque governed by consultation (*shura*) and led by persons accountable to the members of the mosque. Such an arrangement may manifest aspects of the board of directors model and incorporates the consultation (*shura*) element described in the satellite model. An independent local mosque is usually formed by individual Muslims who have expressed dissatisfaction with the other three models described above, and are trying to democratize and Islamicize simultaneously their mode of self-governance. Unwilling to be dominated by a local charismatic Amir or a national/international Islamic movement, members of an independent local mosque usually claim to be faithful followers of the prophetic traditions in their adherence to consultation (*shura*). These members also strongly believe that they should not be dictated to by national or international Muslim groups, for this kind of community is more open to different ideas.

CONCLUSIONS

In conclusion, the patterns of migration of Muslims from the old world to the new world have largely contributed to the emergence of the two main categories of the Muslims in North America—the native-born and the immigrants. These diverse communities are likely to remain unchanged due to the durability of the ethnic, legal schools (*madhabib*) and Sufi path (*tariq*) divides that currently exist in Muslim communities around North America. The third conclusion is that the racialization of Islam among certain elements in Afro-America will continue to strengthen the hands of charismatic figures such as Minister Louis Farrakhan.

A fourth conclusion is that the continued activity of international Muslim groups will reinforce the satellite model of leadership and thus make more difficult efforts at domesticating Muslim centers of religious activity. A fifth conclusion is that the Americanization and democratization of leadership among Muslims in North America is going to depend on the emergence of national organizations founded by groups whose models of leadership are either corporate or consultative (*shuraistic*). By fusing these two elements of leadership together the Muslims of North America may be able to lay the foundation for viable local as well as national Muslim organizations. Last but not least, it can be concluded that the future of the Muslim community is going to depend on the acceptance of the diversity in the community and the realization that Muslims can be effective members of North American society only when they maintain their unity in diversity and maximize their utility in society through individual creativity and moral example.

3
ISLAM AND THE AMERICAN DREAM

A t the beginning of the twentieth century it would have been a joke for someone to tell his friends in America, Europe or the Muslim world that Islam would one day be counted among America's four leading religions. Yet, the train of history has ruled otherwise. Islam today is a vibrant religion, whose "resurgence" is discussed in American newspapers and magazines. It has captured the hearts and loyalty of over one million Americans and immigrants of different races and cultural and national origins. Its followers are now found in almost all levels of American society, although one must hasten to add that it is still a young and struggling faith in a land where the majority belongs to the Christian faith. Islam in the United States must be seen as one religion among a multitude of faiths and beliefs, existing in a society which prides itself on the fact that its traditions and constitution encourage the "separation of church and state." In view of this stress on the separation of religion from the political system, one might wonder whether the arrival of Islam in the United States may have any meaningful impact American society. Another point that deserves some analytical consideration is the relation of Islam to the American dream?

The first Muslim immigrants who came in search of the American dream were from the Mediterranean region of the world. Following the construction of the Suez Canal, and in response to the political unrest developing within the Ottoman Empire, a small but growing number of Syrian and Lebanese Arabs began to seek their fortunes elsewhere. Some of them moved to West Africa, others to South America, and yet some others to the United States. At the beginning of this mass emigration, the majority of the Ottoman Empire were Christian Arabs. With the increase in the number of tales of Arab successes in the United States, many Muslims left the Middle East for the New World. One Lebanese

Muslim, after learning from the captain of the ship bound for United States that there were no mosques in America, quickly jumped off the boat. Such reluctant Muslims were gradually replaced by adventure-some Muslims who came to the United States in the hope of striking it rich quickly, and then returning home. Many of these men never left the United States. Their fates resemble those of latter day Muslim immigrants, who went to England in the fifties and sixties and decided to stay for good. In the case of those who came to America, the decision to stay was occasioned by a new sense of freedom. Many stayed because their American dream of acquiring wealth and property beyond their wildest dreams was realized.

Arab Muslim immigrants settled along the eastern seaboard and in the midwestern parts of the United States. Indeed, the first mosques and Islamic centers in the continental United States were built among the Arab settlers living in the midwest. Also, the first breakthrough of Islam among native born Americans, and particularly Black Americans, took place in the midwest. Despite this midwestern concentration, some of the earliest Muslim organizations, such as the International Muslim Union (1885), the African Moslem Welfare Society of America (founded by Sudanese Imam Muhammad Majid in 1927) and the Muslim Society of the celebrated Muhammad Webb, the American diplomat to the Philippines who later converted to Islam in the 1890's, were based in New York and Pittsburgh. These early organizations, with the exception of Webb's, were primarily made up of immigrant or visiting Muslims.

Between the 1900s and the 1930s, the number of Muslim immigrants began to increase significantly. Muslims of eastern and southern Europe, following the example of their non-Muslim neighbors, began to emigrate to the United States in search of the American dream. These were Albanian and Yugoslavian Muslims who were fleeing from oppressive political situations in their countries. Many of these European immigrants settled in the eastern seaboard and the midwest. There were also Muslim immigrants who came from the Soviet-dominated areas to the north. Some Muslims from Poland have been traced by writers to the descendants of Genghis Khan. They, too, settled in the New York/New Jersey area and carved a place for themselves in the biscuit industry. Immigrants from Ukraine settled in New York City (Brooklyn area) before branching out into neighboring areas. These

Muslims organized themselves into the Mohammedan Society of America which had its headquarters in Brooklyn. An unpublished study done by a Slavic scholar in the United States traced their point of entry into the country to the early twentieth century.

Another group of early Muslim immigrants who came in search of the American dream and later settled in the United States were the Muslims of the Punjab in British India. Following in the footsteps of their Sikh neighbors, these Muslims responded to food shortages in their country at the turn of the century by coming to the United States. They largely settled on the west coast as farm workers; Willows, California was one of their earliest settlements. Today the descendants of these early Muslims are scattered throughout the western United States. Of course, some Pakistani and Indian Muslim immigrants also settled on the eastern seaboard. Like their Muslim and non-Muslim brethren from the non-European world, they were students, seamen, traders and stow-aways who decided to make America their home. Many of them married into American families. The most well-known case of an American-Pakistani marriage is that of Fazal Khan who came to the United States in 1912 and married a Black American woman on the eastern seaboard. His story was reported in the news throughout America because his American daughter, Lurey Khan, following the example of Alex Haley, author of *Roots*, journeyed to Pakistan in search of her roots. There were many cases like that of the Khans, and today in Pennsylvania, Delaware, Maryland and in the New York/New Jersey one can find many descendants of early Muslims among White and Black American families.

One other case which deserves closer attention is the claim of the late Shaykh Daoud Faisal and his wife Sister Khadija. This couple, who founded the Islamic Mission of America, played an important role in the early propagation of Sunni Islam. In a recent interview, Sister Khadija revealed her Pakistani roots by showing photographic evidence of her early life. The offspring of a Pakistani Muslim father and a Black Caribbean mother, she settled in the United States. There she met and married her husband, who was the child of a Moroccan man and a Grenadian woman from the West Indies. These and other unions between Muslim immigrants were brought about by the common search for a new and better life in America. Their common quest for the

American dream brought them together to bring up Muslim children in their new homeland.

In looking into the relation between Islam and the American dream, one can argue that the search for fortune and the realization of dreams motivated many of these early immigrants to plant the seed of their faith in America. In order to survive, these men and women embarked upon new careers and entered into new ventures. Following in the footsteps of many earlier immigrants to the United States, Muslims immigrants engaged in peddling wares in the major cities of the eastern seaboard. Here the early career of the prophet of Islam in trade and commerce provided an example to Muslims trying to earn their keep while simultaneously maintaining their faith in a foreign land. Many Muslim immigrants spoke little or no English at all, and their lives were centered around the small community in which they lived. They often traveled long distances selling goods and merchandise obtained from their fellow countrymen, or from big wholesalers looking for fast profits from the services of recently arrived foreigners. A turn of phrase developed which is still heard today in the northeast and along the eastern seaboard (ranging from Quincy, Massachusetts to Baltimore, Maryland) in which the word "Arab" with an emphasis on the A, is used to refer to street vendors and peddlers. American business historians tell us that foreign-born Americans dominated the field of small business at this time. This is still largely the case because it is the only arena in which they can operate without dealing very intimately with the rest of society. The small business field allows foreigners to avoid discrimination and prejudice at the hands of those who see their poor English and lack of familiarity with Americanisms as a weakness and a liability. Because the Muslim immigrant who was serious about his religion had to pray five times daily at the appointed times for prescribed prayer (*salat*), one could see how peddling became attractive. Not only was it something familiar to Muslims from the east and the old world, but it also granted some leeway to Muslims trying to carve a social and economic niche for themselves in their adopted homeland.

The pattern of peddling which developed along the eastern seaboard was replicated in the midwest. This was an area which attracted the interest and attention of many early Muslim immigrants. Some immigrants in the midwest settled in rural areas where they could obtain land and practice farming; others moved into urban areas where they took up peddling as an occupation; others started to hire themselves out to the emerging motor industry. An entire Arab and Muslim neighborhood developed near auto plants in Highland Park and Hamtramch in Detroit, Michigan. Early in the century, the Muslim segment of this predominantly Arab neighborhood was very small, but as time went on the number of Muslims rose gradually. Letters describing the successful encounters of Arab Muslims with the American dream and the comparative comfort of life in America often started chain migrations. According to the *Detroit Monthly* study two years ago, "over time, almost entire villages were transplanted to the Detroit area. Most of the southern Lebanese here, for example, trace their roots back to two border villages, and there are organizations of Arabs who all come from particular towns, such as Beit Hanina and Ramallah in former Palestine."

It was in the mid-western part of the United States that the mysterious peddler-cum-teacher, Farad Muhammad revealed himself to the late Elijah Muhammad, founder of the Nation of Islam. This powerful organization's early efforts in the name of Islam were denied and rejected by old world Muslims. Later, the movement experienced a radical transformation under the current leader Imam Warith Deen Muhammad. This fundamental change was enacted so that the largest body of Sunni Muslims in the United States more accurately reflected the true teachings of Sunni Islam. Imam Warith Deen Muhammad's actions can be said to be reflective of the contemporary efforts of Muslims to assimilate into mainstream American society and to realize as all other American citizens the fruits and benefits of the American dream. This may sound like an anathema to those who knew the old Nation of Islam (NOI), nevertheless, the American Muslim is currently trying to achieve for its predominantly Black Muslim membership what all the three dominant American religious establishments have done for Protestant, Catholic and Jewish Americans. An interesting point about the American Muslim Mission is that its original founder taught his followers an ethic which has been characterized by some of the American researchers of the movement as "very similar to the work ethic of the Puritans." This work ethic places an emphasis on self-pride and on the dignity of self-help and self-development within the framework of the community. Thus, the teachings of the American Muslim Mission have resulted not in the distancing of the Black Muslim from mainstream

American society but in propelling him toward greater engagement with the American dream. By moving into the field of small business, American Muslim converts became more and more self-confident in their beliefs and in their hopes of realizing their dreams within American society. With this change in perception and attitude came a new feeling that America can be made habitable for all, including Muslims. This attempt to reconcile Islam and the American dream is still in its embryonic stage. A counter-movement, led by a more militant and rebellious group of the old Nation of Islam, is beginning to unfold.

One interesting aspect of Islam in the U. S. is that, until the spring of 1977, there was no national umbrella organization for the many scattered local groups. The Rabatah al-Alam al-Islam (World Muslim League) was able to create such a framework for inter-organizational cooperation at the Newark Conference, and in the 80's a National Council of Imams as well as a Continental Council of Masajid came into being.. With such a system of inter-group cooperation, Muslims will hopefully grapple effectively with the challenges of life in America. In fact, such institutional structures will help Muslims to maintain their identity in the American environment. These umbrella organizations throw up barriers against what Muslims generally consider to be the un-Islamic aspects of modern Western society. Through such organizations, activities such as dancing, drinking and dating American style are banned and discouraged. Though in the past some of these efforts in Muslim communities proved ineffective, the growth in the Muslim population and greater involvement of international Muslim missionary groups such as the Ikhwan al-Muslimoon (Muslim Brotherhood), the Jamiat Al-Islamiyya, the Shia groups, the Tabliqh Movement, the Sufi Brotherhoods and others, have heightened American Muslim consciousness. Their activities have also led to the proliferation of Muslim newspapers, magazines and newsletters. Designed purposely to educate, inspire and inform the members of the Muslim Jamaat, these information services are beginning to forge a sense of strong local and national identity.

The Islamic Jamaat profited greatly from changes introduced by the 1965 Immigration Act. This legislation not only increased the number of Muslims in the general population, but also raised the level of education of the average Muslim immigrant. The liberalization instituted by this Act facilitated the arrival of many professionals from the Arab world, Pakistan, India, Indonesia, Malaysia, Turkey and Iran. In fact, a recent study on Arabs in the U. S. shows that 70 percent of Arabs who came here since 1945 were Muslims. Another phenomenon which followed the passage of the Immigration Act was an increase in the number of Muslim students in the U. S. Whereas in the 1930s, Muslims constituted a negligible portion of the foreign student population, by the late seventies they numbered well over 120,000.

The arrival of Muslims in greater numbers in American society, was made possible by changes in the American immigration laws and by the birth and development of homegrown Islamic movements. The appeal of the American dream, to Muslim immigrants, is neither unique nor peculiar. Most of these men and women were either refugees from oppressive political situations in their own countries, or were lured to America by the greater opportunities of American society. Their case is similar to that of many other immigrants from the old world. The planting of Islam in the United States can be seen as another contribution to the cultural diversity of American society. Writing before the revolutionary changes of the 1960s, Will Herbert could say that, "By and large, to be an American today means to be either Protestant, a Catholic, or a Jew . . .Unless one is either . . .one is 'nothing'; to be a "something', to have a name, one must identify oneself and be identified by others, as belonging to one or another of the three great religious communities in which the American people are divided." Under present conditions and given the gradual growth of Islam among indigenous Americans, one can say that Herbert's statement now needs some revision. The growth of the Arab/Asian immigrant population has swelled the numbers of Buddhist, Sikhs, Bahais, Hindus and of course Muslims living in the U.S.

With the successful planting of Islam in American Society, it is quite conceivable that someday American Muslims could be one of the major pillars of support of world Islam. American Muslim centers, like those of other branches of the Abrahamic tradition, may play an important role in the cultural development of their brethren elsewhere in the Muslim world. All these developments, however, will depend on the success of native-born as well as immigrant Muslims who have opted for American citizenship and strive to see their Muslim dreams wrapped in the greater American dream. Muslims and other American believers in the religious heritage of mankind will maintain and pass on their respective traditions only if they succeed in holding their own against the very powerful forces of secularism and materialism in American society.

4

THE DEVELOPMENT OF MUSLIM INSTITUTIONS IN THE UNITED STATES OF AMERICA

Islam is now one of the three major religions in the United States. This fact is not widely appreciated in the larger society, but scholars and journalists have continued to remind the American society that the Muslims are here and their presence can be gauged and ascertained by their institutions and by the actions which these institutions have undertaken in order to assimilate into the larger U. S. cultural landscape. From sociological and anthropological literature we learn that human groups are able to transmit cultures and values across time and space due to the processes of institution-building and socialization. By such mechanisms, human beings have, from the beginning of time, managed to raise generation after generation on a steady diet of culture and tradition. Religions have been center pieces in such enterprises, and scholarly writings have all credited Christianity in Europe and Islam in the Muslim world with the humanization of the animal instinct through the inculcation of values about the human being, family, society, history and responsibility beyond the grave goes with Muslims wherever their business travel or missionary work take them. In a society like the U. S., where Muslims number at least five million, it is apparent that this long history of socialization of the member of the Muslim Community (*ummah*) travels with the Muslims wherever their business or missionary work takes them. It is essential for them to engage in the process of institution building in order for them to survive in their new home, with their new approach to life, their new lifestyles, and their recent restoration to their true nature (*fitra*). They must build Islamic schools to teach their children; they must provide religious instruction to their veteran

55

members as well as to their new members of the faith; they must set up structures to the same sorts of issues which older religious groups with greater heritages have already dealt with over time. Critical in the development of these institutions are the mosques (*masajid*), the governing council (*Majlis al-shura*), financial structures to facilitate the buying of property without paying usurious interest (*riba*), the establishment of Alms (*zakah*) and the disbursement of such funds to the different groups of beneficiaries, as stipulated in Shariah; the establishment of regular prayer, especially Friday (*jumah*), and Festival (*id*) prayers; the appointment of Imams and the institutionalization of Imamate under various guises; the establishment of standard Islamic procedures for Funeral (*janazah*) prayer and the burial of deceased Muslims; the establishment of abattoirs for the slaughtering of livestock in accordance with Islamic principle; the establishment of *halal* (permissible) meat markets and the organization of pilgrims for the annual pilgrimage to Mecca and Medina in Saudi Arabia.

The purpose of this essay is to trace briefly the history of the Muslim community in the U.S. and to identify the various institutional structures they have created over the years in their attempt to maintain their Din and to adjust to the demands and challenges of U.S. society. While pursuing this task, efforts will be made to trace the historical evolution of such institutions and the forces and factors responsible for their development.

THE ADVENT OF ISLAM IN THE U. S. AND ITS PATTERNS OF DEVELOPMENT

In tracking the historical record of Islam in the U.S., five phases in the evolution of the Muslim community can be identified. The first phase, which is speculative, not well documented and a bit controversial, deals with the Pre-Columbian past, while the second phase covers the period when the Atlantic Slave Trade was in effect, importing African slaves to work on American plantations. The third of these phases deals with the immigration of Muslims from the Old World to the New World, followed by the fourth phase dealing with the rise of Islam among American citizens and the influence of the native-born Muslims in the development of Islam in North America. And finally, the fifth phase brings us to the 1990's, to a period where Muslim numbers have increased dramatically, augmenting the visibility of its institutions due to wider coverage by the media.

THE PRE-COLUMBIAN MUSLIM PRESENCE IN THE AMERICAS

The first scholar to provide the scholarly community with some data concerning possible Muslim presence in Meso-America was Harvard University Professor Leo Weiner. Writing over seventy years ago, Weiner presented evidence available to him through his linguistic and ethnological studies of Native American groups in Mexico. Central to his thesis is that Arabic and Mande-speaking peoples from the North Western part of the African continent traveled by sea and established contact with local peoples of the Mexican Coast. In identifying a number of the languages of the Mexican native people words (similar to the Muslim counterparts) he illustrated intercultural borrowings between the two cultures.

Over the last two decades, Wiener's views have been reinforced by the works of Ivan Van Sertima. Using Wiener's findings as a stepping stone, Van Sertima has brought to light historical data from various sources in the Caribbean and the other parts of the Americas that maintain the argument that black Africans (though not limited to Muslims) came to the New World before Christopher Columbus.

Wiener and Van Sertima's view also has received support from African historians like Basil Davidson, who has quoted translations of Al-Omari's account on the possible Malian expedition across the Atlantic Ocean in order to defend this theory. According to this Arab source of the Medieval period of Mediterranean history, King Abu bakr the first, of the Mali Empire, dispatched a large contingent of canoes equipped with adequate provisions for his sailors to ply the Atlantic Ocean and establish ties with the indigenous peoples of the New World.

Examining these three different sources regarding the possible contact between Muslims and peoples of the New World, one can conclude that the evidence provided is not of substantial strength or depth to prove that Muslim institutions were established or that natives of contemporary Mexico have residues of Islam and Muslims in their cultures.

THE MUSLIM SLAVES AND DEVELOPMENT
OF ISLAMIC INSTITUTIONS

The Atlantic Slave Trade brought millions of African slaves to the New World, though historians disagree on the exact number of those who landed in the New World. But nonetheless, the fact remains that at least a conservative figure of ten million slaves came across its Middle Passage. According to Allan Austin, whose African Muslims in Ante Bellum America has collected a majority of the important literary fragments regarding Muslim slaves in the U.S, at least ten percent of the slaves who arrived in the U.S. were Muslims. Profiles of several of these Muslim slaves show that they tried desperately to hold on to their Muslim faith. However, the hostile environment of North American Slavery, separating family members from each other and denying the African Slave, regardless of religious practice, the freedom and the opportunity to practice his right to worship made it impossible for the Muslims to pass their religion to their children. Due to the fact that slaves were not deemed human, it was often forgotten that they too could be creators and custodians of cultures worth preserving. As a result, the accounts we have about Muslim slaves only vaguely describe any meaningful efforts to establish a stable institution. Maintenance of the Islamic identity was attempted through different means; including the insistence on one's original Muslim name; the retention of Quranic knowledge; and the conferring of Muslim names to one's children.

One such account is related to us by the American artist David Willson Peale regarding the life of Yarrow Mamout. What makes Yarrow's story fascinating to students of early Muslim life in the United States of America is that, though he was not married and did not have a family, considered the primary unit of human institution-building, he persevered during his lifetime to honor and live by the Islamic precepts. Maintaining the Muslim dietary practice, he told the butchers of Georgetown in Washington, D.C. that he did not eat pork, and he also took to heart the Quranic injunction that believers are to do the dhikr (celebrating praises to Allah) and remember their Creator.

A similar example comes from the American experiences of Ayub Ibn Sulayman Diallo, better known as Job Ben Solomon, a prince from Bondu in modern day Guinea Conakry. Here again, an individual Muslim is confronted with the challenges of operating in an alien environment without any reinforcing cultural institutions. What Douglas

Grant tells us in his *The Fortune Slave* is that Job insisted on saying his five daily prayers and his dedication was so intense that he was able to recite the entire Quran from memory. Facing many odds, Job attempted to reproduce the Quranic school environment in his new home of Annapolis, Maryland, where he tried to survive both as a man of royal dignity as well as a Muslim living under captivity.

A third example of this intense devotion comes to us from Fayetteville, North Carolina. Omar Ibn Sayyid, an African slave, lived here after fleeing his original place of captivity and he desperately tried to hold onto to his Islamic identity in spite of the hostile environment which denied him his humanity as well as his right to worship as a Muslim. In the absence of a family and without a community of believers freely practicing their faith, it was impossible for Omar to successfully maintain his religion and organize an Islamic mode of life. Indeed, the predicament of Omar captures John Doone's famous statement that "no man is an island." Omar Ibn Sayyid could not, by himself, be an island of Islamic faith without others to reinforce his identity. This solitary existence leads one to understand why toward the end of his life, Omar had to succumb to the pressure and convert to Christianity.*

The last profile is that of another prince who came from Futa Jallon and Guinea country. Known to historians as Abdurahaman (should read Abdur Rahman), this African prince was captured in battle and sold into slavery. He and his family survived as slaves to a Mr. Forster for forty years until Abdur Rahman managed to obtain his freedom by writing a letter, in Arabic, addressed to the Sultan of Morocco. Abdur Rahman's letter was smuggled by the American Colonization Society and delivered to the Sultan of Morocco, who then intervened on behalf of Abdur Rahman causing the U.S. President Adams to permit his release.

What we learn from this story told in detail by Terry Afford in his *Prince Among Slaves*, is that during his forty years of captivity, Abdur Rahman resisted any imposition of slave names, a pattern that Alex Haley described in his saga of Kunta Kinteh, another Muslim slave from the same region. The evidence available in Alford's study points to the fact since no Islamic reinforcing institutions were permitted to exist, Islam could not be passed across generations, thus Muslim slaves like Abdur Rahman could only preserve their identity by insisting that their African-derived Muslim names remain. Elements which are also critical in Muslim identity formation are consciousness of being a Muslim and the command of written Arabic, both of which played a part in the Saga of Abdur Rahman.

THE INSTITUTION-BUILDING EFFORTS OF MUSLIM IMMIGRANTS IN THE LATE 19TH AND 20TH CENTURY

Muslim immigrants started to come to the U.S. after the construction of the Suez Canal due to the greater percentage of American vessels in what is now called the Middle East. Following the footsteps of the Christian neighbors who had already emigrated to the U.S. and were sending glowing accounts of their success stories. The first wave of Muslims to land on these shores were those from that part of the Ottoman Empire we now call Mount Lebanon.

Muslim Arabs arrived and immediately settled among the Eastern seaboard. Engaged in peddling, many later moved out of the East coast and settled in the midwestern parts of the U.S. There some of them took up farming while others went to work in factories. Populations like Dearborn, Michigan filled with Arabs from Palestine, Syria, Yemen and Lebanon as a result of this pattern of migration.

Coming as students, political refugees, or just visitors not intending to stay in the United States permanently, Arab-Muslim emigrants from Egypt, Iraq and North Africa started to swell the ranks of earlier generations of Arabs in the post war period. Today the total number of Arab Americans reaches over three million, with an estimated 750,000 Muslims included in that figure. However, prior to the Post War period, Muslims were estimated to be only one-tenth of the total Arab population. But, with the liberalization of the U.S. immigration laws under the Johnson administration in the 1960's, and the heightening of political tensions in the Middle East, Muslims have constituted the largest numbers of Arabs coming to the U.S. and Canada, explaining the growth of the Muslim population as a whole, and more particularly the Arab-Muslim population.

The second group of Muslims to emigrate to the U.S. were the South Asians. Following the footsteps of their Sikh neighbors in British India Punjabi Muslims began to come to the western part of the U.S. in the late nineteenth century. Traveling by way of the Philippines, these Punjabis settled in California and British Columbia. Working on the farmlands of the West coast and hoping to earn enough to return home, many of these emigrants became permanent residents of the United States. This pattern of settlement laid the foundation for what one now called the South Asian Muslim presence in the West coast.

After World War II, the numbers of South Asian Muslim emigrants increased. Many South Asian students entered the U.S. under various Cold War-driven U.S. scholarship programs, and some of these students decided to stay on for either political or economic reasons. Among these South Asians who came to Canada and the U.S. were the Sub-Continent people also known as the Hyderabadis, many of whom were professionals who first immigrated to the United Kingdom or to Canada before settling in the U.S. A change in U.S. immigration laws in 1964 allowed the Hyderabadis as well as other South Asians to sponsor family members and relatives to join them in the United States. As a result of this change in U.S. immigration law a large number of professionals in various branches of the physical and natural sciences emigrated to the U.S., creating large populations of South Asian Muslims in Silicon Valley and around many scientific and medical centers of the U.S and Canada.

Besides the Arabs and the South Asians, there were also Muslim immigrants who came from Southern Europe, the Middle East, Central Asia as well as other areas of the Muslim World. The Southern European Muslims mostly from the Province of Bosnia in the old Republic of Yugoslavia, were descendants of Serbo-Croatian speaking people who had embraced Islam several centuries ago. These Bosnian Muslims arrived in the U.S. following the footsteps of their Christian neighbors who had emigrated there a decade or two earlier. Settling along the Eastern seaboard, many of them engaged in petty trade and small business while a larger number sought employment in American factories. In addition to the Bosnians, there were also the Albanian Muslims and a tiny fraction of Polish Muslims, identified by historians as descendants of Genghis Khan.

Muslims also emigrated from Ukraine in the former Soviet Union and settled in the New York City area and in its neighboring states. Fleeing from the tyranny of communist rule in Central Asia, more Muslims from the former Soviet Empire emigrated hoping to start a new life in the U.S. many of whom found new homes along the eastern seaboard. Many of them had fled to Turkey before deciding to seek asylum in the U.S. This inter-war wave of Turkish-speaking immigrants was later reinforced by the post war emigration of Turkish Muslims. As stated earlier in connection with Arab and South Asian Muslims' immigration, it should be pointed out here that Turkish-speaking immigrants came to the United States as foreign students under Cold War-driven programs. Many of these students for one reason or another decided to remain permanently in the U.S. and as a result sizable Muslim Turkish community exists along the Eastern seaboard.

The communist takeover of the Persian-speaking region of Central Asia and the influx of Iranians fleeing from the regime of the Shah resulted in a settlement of Persian-speaking people from Central Asia and Iraq in the U.S. And then, following the collapse of the Shah's regime and the installation of the Khomeini regime, the number of Iranian immigrants increased. Today the Muslims of Iranian descent are found primarily in California as well as along the Eastern seaboard.

Muslims from other parts of the world include Southeast Asian Muslims, Caribbean Muslims, West-African Muslims, and Muslims from island states on the Indian and Pacific oceans. The first Southeast Asian Muslims to set foot in the U.S were the Yunnan Chinese Muslims who were part of the Kuomintang army of General Chang Kia-Chek. Many of these Chinese Muslims fled to northern Thailand where they settled in the Changrai area, while some of their better educated numbers left the area and emigrated to the U.S. Many of these Yunnan Chinese Muslims have settled on the West coast and in the Chicago area.

Other Southeast Asian Muslims are the Vietnamese, the Cambodian and the Philippino Muslims. The Muslims from Vietnam, generally known as the Champa Muslims, are from the Muslim enclave in the old Vietnam Kingdom before colonialism and communist rule. These Vietnamese Muslims, however, only constitute a very small fraction of the total Vietnamese population in the U.S. Arriving as what U.S. journalists called the "Boat People," many of them are now part of the large Asian population on the West coast as well as in Northern Virginia.

The small population of Cambodian Muslims living in the U.S. entered as refugees, escaping from their chaos-ridden homeland in Southeast Asia. Many of these Muslims, like others from their country, found a new life in the U.S., more specifically in California and along the eastern seaboard.

The Philippino Muslims who are mainly from Mindanao are also found primarily in the West Coast. Constituting a small fraction of the total Filipino population on the West coast, these Muslims are indistinguishable from the less economically successful Filipinos in the U.S.

Muslim immigrants from West Africa have decided to settle in the U.S. over the last twenty-five years. Up until the mid 1970's, Africans were not well disposed to emigrate to the U.S. As a result of this change in their attitude, due to political and economic factors, we now witness an increase in the number of Africans, Muslims and non-Muslims, coming to the U. S. with the specific purpose of permanent residency. The crises in Somalia, Sudan and Ethiopia have led to a large number of Muslims desiring to leave the Horn of Africa. There are also the Muslims from Eastern Africa, most of whom are of South Asian descent or of Afro-Arab Swahili cultural background. Those of South Asian descent are most often identified with the Ismaili or other Shia subdivisions in the Muslim World, while those of Afro-Arab Swahili cultural background are immigrants who fit into the pattern of settlement indirectly linked to, and brought about by the Post War phenomenon of international student exchange programs organized by the U.S. during the Cold War. Some of these Muslims, however, were the victims of political persecution at the hands of former Ugandan dictator Idi Amin Dada. As a part of the Asian population forcefully ejected by Amin, a shameful act now immortalized for Americans in the Hollywood production of Mississippi Masala, these East African Muslims are now found in Canada and the U.S.

In addition to the West Africans, the Muslims of the Horn of Africa and the Muslims of East Africa there are also the Muslims from South Africa. A small percentage of the South African apartheid refugees, these Muslims are mainly business people, a significant portion of whom are in jewelry and gold trading.

There are also Muslims from some of the islands of the Indian and Pacific Oceans. Several Muslim families from Fiji are now located on the West coast of the U.S, more specifically in the San Francisco Bay area. Being of Indian sub-continent origin, most of these Muslims were lured into immigration by the earlier settlement by Muslims from Punjab.

Besides Fiji, there are Muslims from Mauritius, Maldives and Sri Lanka who form part of the Muslim community in the U.S. Mostly of South Asian descent these immigrants form separate and distinct communities from Indians, Pakistanis and Bangladeshis.

A similar pattern of settlement in the U. S. is evident in the Muslim communities of the Caribbean immigrants. Most Muslim immigrants from this part of the world are of Indian or of Afro-Indian descent.

Proud of their distinct ethnic background and committed to their unique Muslim identity in a Caribbean world dominated by Christianity, these Muslims from Guyana, Trinidad and Jamaica carry double identities. Their non-Urdu-speaking background clearly demarcates them from persons from South Asia, despite the physical resemblance, while their strong identification with Islam distinguishes them from the Black Caribbeans with whom they share a common language.

The Caribbean Muslim community is gradually expanding to embrace new members from the black population of many islands. The small but vibrant Muslim community in Bermuda is a good example of this. Though the numbers of this population are minimal, the fact remains that some of its members now live on the U.S. mainland as immigrants. This is true for Muslim immigrants of African descent from other islands of the Caribbean as well. While some of these persons were Muslims before they came to the U.S., others discovered Islam upon arrival.

Though these various immigrant groups come from distinct homelands, together they comprise the larger Muslim community. In order to survive in the U.S., this community had to focus on institution-building, a three stage process which each of these individual Muslim communities had to endure.

During the late nineteenth and early twentieth century no serious effort of institution-building was undertaken by any of the immigrant groups. We have evidence of an international Islamic organization located in New York towards the end of the 1890's. What we do not know is the nature of its operation or the degree of its success. One can speculate that the founders of such an organization were either part of a small body of Muslim business people living and working in New York City or they were some of the earliest Muslim immigrants from the Ottoman Empire and Southern Europe who bonded together with their native born American co-religionists, because it is assumed that Muhammad Alexander Russell Webb, the first known American believer in Islam, was linked to the organization.

However, Muhammad's institution-building efforts among immigrants in the United States did not manifest itself until the first three decades of the twentieth century. The first established Friday prayer took place, not in New York city where the earliest Muslims had landed and settled, but rather in Ross, North Dakota. Nor was the first constructed mosque built in the east coast, but instead in Detroit, Michigan. According to FBI records, the Muslims of Pittsburgh, who at the time were suspected to be the subject of political manipulation by Japanese agents in the black and Arab communities of that city, established a school where the Quran and the Arabic language were taught. The record further shows that a Sudanese Imam was imported by the Pittsburgh Muslims in 1927, but he left in the following year.

Institution-building among the immigrants did not lead to greater Islamization. Up until the post war period, no evidence exists to show serious Muslim initiative to establish such institutions. For instance, the mosque built in the 1920's by Muslims in Detroit with the generous financial assistance of a Syrian businessman was closed down because of disagreement between the Qadiyani Muslims from British India (considered unorthodox and heretical by other Muslims in the subcontinent) and the predominantly Arab Muslims (who rejected the leadership of the followers of Mirza Ghulam Ahmad, the self-declared Mahdi of the 19th century).

The influx of international Muslim students during the cold war and the tide of Arab nationalism championed by Gamal Abdul Nasser of Egypt resulted in Muslim immigrants becoming more involved in institution-building. In his book, Arab Moslems of the United States of America, Professor Abdo El-Kholy explains that the Federation of Islamic Associations (FIA) was formed in the early 1950's and that these Arab Muslim members were influenced by the same sense of pride that accompanied Nasser's Pan Arabism. Although the FIA predated the Egyptian Revolution by one year, there is evidence to support El-Kholy's contention that the FIA leaders saw the resurgence of Arab nationalism as reason for their acknowledgment and development of their Arab and Islamic heritage. In order to achieve this goal, these Arab Muslims formed an umbrella organization to give national visibility to their various members.

Institution-building efforts at the national level were made possible by the existence of Muslim communities in Toledo, Ohio, Dearborn, Michigan, Cedar Rapids, Iowa, and in several cities along the eastern seaboard. In each of these communities, Muslim families, and in particular, Arab families, tried to socialize their children into Islamic culture and to build up the necessary institutional structures to pass across time and space the intellectual and spiritual heritage of Islam.

The lack of substantial knowledge regarding Islam among first and especially second generation Arab Muslims caused community leaders in many instances to recruit what we now call the "imported Imam." Brought in purposely to lead prayers, give religious instructions and teach the young children, this "imported Imam" was expected to play a substantial role in the institution-building efforts of the Arab Muslim communities, though this role was destined to be only partially fulfilled due to the poor understanding of U.S. society and culture on the part of such Imams. According to El-Kholy, the institution-building exercise was further complicated by the assimilation process which separated the first and the second generation of Muslim immigrants. Born into U.S. society and culture, and subject to on-going Americanization, most if not all of the second generation Muslim Arabs had some difficulty with the rigidities in Islamic practice ordered or taught by their imported Imams. It is these differential attitudes in El-Kholy's view, that are clearly demonstrated in the differences between the Muslims of Toledo, Ohio and the Muslims of Dearborn, Michigan. Whereas in Toledo the Muslims took a very liberal view of religion, like that of a second generation Muslim, those living in Dearborn tended to be more conservative and strict like a first generation Muslim.

These different patterns of institution-building were destined to impact the future course of Muslim institution-building in the U.S. as a whole. The first evidence of this tension was the decision by Muslim international students in U.S. colleges and universities to create organizations which were separate and distinct from the existing ones run by the Arab Muslim immigrants. Since these international students were coming from Arab, Iranian and South Asian communities where Islamic reform groups were locked in battle against secular nationalist movements such as Nasserism, the founding fathers of what later emerged as the Muslim Student Association (M.S.A) found the type of Islam practiced by the earlier generation of immigrants tainted by secularism and materialism.

In hope of protecting themselves from the dangerous virus of secularism and materialism, these students, who back home were affiliated with or at least supported the efforts of the Muslim Brotherhood of Hassan al-Banna and Syed Qutb or the Jamiati Islami of Maulana Mawdudi or the Ayatollahs working with Ayatollah Quwi of Najaf in Iraq, designed the MSA to serve their specific purposes. Meeting in places like Gary and Indianapolis, Indiana in 1963-64 academic year and determined to build up a Muslim organization as strong as the one created by Muslim students in England, the leaders of this Muslim Student Movement soon moved their operations to neighboring universities in Gary, Indiana and finally to Plainfield, Indiana, where their large headquarters stands as a monument to their collective efforts. This location served as the nexus of Muslim energy designed to help set up MSA chapters across the U.S. and Canada. Between 1963-64 and 1979-80 the MSA succeeded in creating a network of over 120 chapters on both American and Canadian campuses. Today there are many fully equipped student mosques in places like Madison, Wisconsin, Tempe, Arizona, Syracuse, New York and Columbia, Missouri, to name just a few. Many of these structures, built over the last twenty years, were the result of generous assistance from rich benefactors from the petrodollar states in the Middle East.

Immigrant mosque-building efforts were not limited to U.S. and Canadian campuses. As pointed out earlier many Muslims who had come to the U. S. and Canada to study, decided to remain here permanently. Concerned about the fate of their children and the future of Islam in North America, many of these Muslims, now professionals in the U. S. and Canadian job market, created community centers and mosques. It is largely due to their efforts and those of the native-born American Muslims that North American Muslims today can count at least one thousand five hundred mosques and Islamic centers as evidence of their institutional and cultural presence in this part of the world.

5

CONVERGENCE AND DIVERGENCE IN AN EMERGENT COMMUNITY: A STUDY OF CHALLENGES FACING U.S. MUSLIMS

INTRODUCTION

Since the last three decades of the nineteenth century Muslims have been voluntarily immigrating to the United States. While many of these men came to these shores with the specific objective of striking it rich just to return home to lead more attractive and more comfortable lives, a few were businessmen who journeyed to America to sample some of her wares and then to return home to sell whatever their fancy let them purchase. However, this kind of visitor was rare and his example was to remain unimitated on a large scale, until the post-war period.

But Islam's identity in the United States as a whole is not only defined by immigrants searching for economic opportunities in a strange land, but also comprises the experience of conversion by a small but growing body of indigenous men and women in American society who discovered a new way of life and a new belief system that filled, and continues to fill a void in their spiritual lives. Students visiting the United States have also subscribed to and supported Islam since the 1930's.

Comprised, since its initial conception, of different racial, ethnic, and social groups, the Muslim community in the United States faced many different challenges with regards to its development. The main difference among the immigrants, the native-born and the converted Muslims was their sectarian interpretations of the Quran and of the life and example of the Holy Prophet Muhammad. However, the racial

69

question, a perpetual and significant confrontation in America, has continued to serve as a wedge between the followers of the Nation of Islam and other heterodox groups, particularly those with some elements of Islam in their statement of beliefs or formulation of rituals, and the orthodox Muslims. This American dilemma, reflected in the microcosm of the Muslim community "manifested itself in the early encounter between immigrant Islam and local conditions in American society."[1]

The different reactions to the challenges and opportunities in American society can be described as either Elijahian or Webbian approaches to Islamic propagation (dawah) in American society.[2] An approach is considered Elijahian when it follows the teachings of Elijah Muhammad regarding the effective and rigid separation of the races and an approach is known as Webbian when it takes Muhammad Alexander Russell Webb's view of Islam as a color-blind religion, addressing itself to the plight of all people in the world. The evolution of both the immigrant and indigenous segments of the Muslim Community (ummah) in the United States reveals these two distinct tendencies. Whereas the majority of the indigenous and immigrant Muslims embraced an Islam which is color-blind, there remained a pocket of heterodox and sometimes orthodox Sunni Muslims, especially in Afro-America, who saw Islam as an ideological weapon in the fight against white racism.[3]

In this paper our attention will be focused on the emerging Muslim community—now comprised of two basic constituent groups of immigrants from virtually all parts of the Muslim world and native-born Americans, converts to the faith of Islam, the Muslim community is now estimated to be about five million.[4] The history of this emerging Muslim community dates back to the 19th century. However, Islam among Americans as a national phenomenon did not occur until the 1960's.

The challenges facing the Muslims in the U. S. can be traced back to the 19th century. Our task here is to show how these challenges affect the nature of Muslim life in the U. S. and the responses of the Muslim Community (ummah) to these challenges. Working on the assumption that the Muslim community is not a monolithic group, and taking note of the fact that both the indigenous and the immigrant segments of the Muslim community respond differently to some of the challenges facing Muslims, this paper argues that the different degrees of assimilation to American culture and society have profoundly affected the entire U. S.

Muslim community. The challenges which this study addresses are the following:
(1) The challenge to maintain an Islamic identity.
(2) The challenge to project and defend Islamic institutions.
(3) The challenge to build Muslim economic structures.
(4) The challenge to participate in American political life.

CHALLENGE TO MAINTAIN ISLAMIC IDENTITY

The most crucial element in the history and development of a social group is the maintenance of its identity. American Muslims live in a country where identification is defined politically, linguistically, culturally and ethnically. First of all a U. S. citizen in the eyes of the Muslim world, his fellow Americans look upon him as a member of a racial group. He is further classified culturally and religiously. Although American social scientists speak much about the civic religion that now dominates the larger American society, the political and cultural pluralism to which it gives rise does not put an end to the feelings and perceptions of religious identity and affiliation, particularly among American Muslims. Accordingly, the American Muslim must recognize that he lives in four concentric circles in order to define properly and to maintain effectively a strong identity. He is a U. S. citizen whose political loyalty is to these United States and he affirms this in a number of ways. Examples of this commitment to the American identity include the Muslim's acceptance of all duties expected of all citizens—including service in the armed forces—and his assertion of his rights guaranteed by the U. S. Constitution, such as the bold assertion of the freedom of speech to do propagation (*dawah*) for Islam.

But while pointing to the first circle of identity of the American Muslim, let us not forget that the American Muslim, whether indigenous or naturalized, also lives in other circles of identification. Without his constant mindfulness of the non-racial nature of Islam, the American Muslim, by virtue of his early conditioning in a racially conscious society, could easily become trapped in a world of racial consciousness which cuts him off from other Muslims in different racial groups. This is a major challenge to the emerging Muslim Community (*ummah*). Ironically, this is also one of the most American aspects of American Islam, for many other American religions are also still grappling with this racial problem. Because Muslim Americans are neither racially homogeneous nor ethnically monolithic, one wonders how the Muslim leadership will build the necessary bridges within its own community to spare the Muslim Americans the racial divide that presently splits the other Abrahamic religions. These groups—islands of ethnicity and race—seemingly find themselves united by mere threads—a distant past and by a common prayer for a united eschatological destiny. Islam hopes to pay more than just lip service to the goal of a single world religion.

The third circle of identity of the American Muslim is shaped by his ethnic origin. For him, this means not only common national origin and/or racial identity, but also a third factor: ethnic consciousness. This ethnic consciousness within the Muslim community is a subtler form of differentiation, particularly among the immigrant Muslims. It manifests itself only as the number of Muslims from abroad increases and the process of self-identification and self-differentiation begins to emerge. For example, as the number of Arabic-speaking members of a Muslim community increases, a natural segmentation or grouping along national lines occurs. The Syrians begin to branch off from the Egyptians, the Saudis from the Moroccans. Among the South Asians, the Bengalis regroup themselves from other South Asians as their numbers increase. Many Muslim observers of the American scene argue that such clustering is uniquely American. It is not. Muslim leaders should recognize that this human tendency is neither a setback nor un-Islamic. To the contrary: used positively, the ethnic differences within the Muslim Community (*ummah*) might help to create the bridges between leaders and members of such groups that will make a workable, united Islam possible.

The Muslim identity in the U. S. must also be defined in terms of the sociological realities of American society as a whole. To illustrate the challenge of such a definition, we will take a close look at ethnicity in the Muslim segment of the African-American community. In this part of American society, ethnicity is virtually synonymous with race. This peculiar situation has primarily emerged among converts to Islam through two tendencies: the assimilationist and the simulationist views of Islamization. The assimilationist approach makes the American Muslim convert change his way of life totally. He adopts an Islamic name, Islamic dress reflecting the cultural origins of those who introduced him to Islam, an Islamic code of ethics, and perhaps most importantly, an Islamic consciousness, which negates a great deal of what he has previously been socialized to accept as American culture. Under these conditions, the assimilationist African-American Muslim begins to equate his membership in the Muslim community as an alternative, and sometimes superior, identity to his original ethnic identity. Such a person, depending on several factors which contribute to his self-definition, may now see a conflict between his Islamic and his American identities. This psychological type, however, is not the sole model of assimilationist African-American Muslims. Others are more able to reconcile their Islamic identity with the secular culture, which American sociologist called Americanity. There is also the assimilationist who totally assimilates himself into Islamic culture but still recognizes his Afro-American identity. Though he now sees himself as a part of a subculture within the Afro-American community, he identifies totally with that community in matters unrelated to religion. Such a person usually has a Muslim name and is active in African-American community life. A third psychological type assimilates totally into the Islamic culture but, for a variety of reasons, opts for the Americanization of his Islamic culture. To put it another way, this type of African-American Muslim, by virtue of his previous positive attitudes toward American culture and American constitutionalism, sees his new Muslim identity as a way of shedding what he perceives as negative characteristics of his past identity in America. Such a person usually has a Muslim first name and an American last name.

By contrast, simulationists take a totally different view of Islam. While they are willing to embrace this new religion, their decision to do so is largely determined by utilitarian considerations which grow out of their experiences in American society. They usually see Islam as a political weapon, a strategy for physical and spiritual survival, and a way of life that could be effectively appropriated in their struggle for racial justice and ethnic freedom in America. The simulationist is prepared to simulate everything within the Muslim community so long as his purpose of self-definition is served. Like the assimilationist he adopts an Islamic name, an Islamic code of dress (notice that it is not an assimilationist mode of dress), an Islamic orthodox or sometimes heterodox view of the world. What however differentiates the simulationist from his assimilationist brethren is his view and use of Islam in American society. Unlike the assimilationists, who can be called Webbian, the simulationists are Elijahian in many respects. But in saying this one must quickly add that not all simulationists are heterodox in their belief and practice of Islam. Just as in the assimilationist group the simulationists are also differentiated. Two types can be identified. First, there is the simulationist who redefined his African-American identity in such a way that his new religion makes him different and separate from both the Muslim community and his fellow African-Americans of non-Islamic faith. This was the nature of the relationship between the Nation of Islam and the Afro-American community on the one hand and the Muslim community on the other. This state of affairs continued up to the transformation effected by Imam Warith Deen Muhammad in the late 1970s. The second group of simulationists consists of those who embrace Islam as a religion, while still insisting strongly on a black nationalism that calls for the unity of all black people regardless of religion.

In looking at the evolution of the Nation of Islam one notices the transformation of that movement from a simulationist group with a heterodox interpretation of Islam to a *bona fide* Muslim group with an assimilationist philosophy of Islamism and Americanism.[5] In fact, one can argue that this movement, which the late Honorable Elijah Muhammad (1897-1975) inherited from Abdul Wali Farad Muhammad Ali (1897-1929?) in the 1930s, has spawned elements which can now be identified with both the assimilationists and the simulationists. Two of the major groups which now claim the legacy of Honorable Elijah Muhammad are the former American Muslim Mission of Imam Warith Deen Muhammad and the reconstituted Nation of Islam under Minister Louis Farrakhan, both of which are good examples of the assimilationist and simulationist views of Islam.

THE CHALLENGE TO BUILD AND DEFEND ISLAMIC INSTITUTIONS

In looking at the challenges facing the emergent Muslim Community (*ummah*) in America, one finds that second only to the identity question is the challenge to build and defend Islamic institutions. Muslims have been aware of this since the early years of their sojourn in the United States and both Muslim immigrants and native-born Muslims have tackled this question. The limited historical record of early Muslims in the U. S. shows that several hurdles impeded the Muslims' attempt to establish institutions within their community. First of all, most of the Muslim people who eventually became immigrants arrived without any definite sense of permanency regarding their stay in the U. S. Consumed with the goals of striking it rich quickly and returning home at the earliest opportunity, their minds were not focused on institution-building. Not to mention the fact that, the over-whelming majority were illiterates. Thus the intellectual and social resources necessary for dealing with the challenges of building institu-tions remained unavailable. This clear lack of literate and responsible leadership among the early Muslims accounted for the postponement of effective institution-building.

Efforts towards Muslim institutions were half-hearted and sporadic. Organizations were formed to deal with such needs, but their brief exis-tence and collapse testified to the poor state of organization among Muslims. In Ross, North Dakota where historians of Islam in America now identify the first Friday congregational prayer (jummah) in that city as the oldest in America,[6] a small Muslim community thrived for a while. Pittsburgh, Pennsylvania was the birthplace of the African Muslim Welfare Association of North America (AMWANA)[7] and in the late 1920s this early Muslim organization set about building Muslim institutions for its members living in the city. With a Sudanese Muslim serving for a short while as the Imam in this Pittsburgh community, AMWANA tried to teach Arabic to its members and to provide them with basic instructions on Islam. By the late 1930s, the collective efforts of the Arabs, Serbians, Turks, Bosnians, Albanians, Ukrainians and indige-nous African-Americans who settled in the eastern seaboard of the U. S. and in the Midwest laid the foundations for a Muslim Community (ummah).

The arrival of the South Asian Muslims of the Ahmadiyyat Movement to America, which settled in Chicago, was a major challenge to American Muslims, particularly to those Arab Americans who felt that their leadership was being threatened by a heterodox group of South Asian Muslims. This new arrival in the American religious land-scape was destined to interact with many African-Americans. The Ahmadiyyat Movement's activities in Chicago and Detroit linked some of its early African-American converts to the Nation of Islam.[8] But while admitting the fact that in the 1920s the United States of America wit-

nessed the planting of orthodox, and not so orthodox Islam in the midwest, the fact still remains that advocates of Islam among southern
European and middle eastern Muslims demonstrated nothing but weakness in their efforts at Muslim institution-building.

The period beginning with the end of World War II serves as a new
chapter in Muslim efforts at institution-building. Two factors caused
changes in Muslim self-perception as well as in Muslim strategies for
institution-building. The first was the decision of a group of second
generation Arab Muslims and their co-religionists from elsewhere in
Darul Islam to organize a national organization. This plan to organize
nationally resulted from the impact of events in the Middle East on
Arab-Americans, both Christian and Muslim, and the gradual but
strong popularity of Gamal Abdul Nasser in Arab communities in
America. As Professor Abdo El-Kholy pointed out, the message of Nasser,
which aroused Arab consciousness concerning the Palestinian debate,
was present in all Arab communities causing many Arab-Americans to
take pride in their heritage and to pay greater attention to events in that
part of the world.[9]

The second factor affecting Muslim-institution building was the
emergence of a small but growing body of students from the Muslim
world who started their academic sojourn in the U. S. in the early 1930s.
Most of these early students were adventurous young men from colo-
nized regions of Darul Islam where bright young men and women
aspired to secure places in British or European universities and colleges.
What increased the number of these students was the direction of world
events after the defeat of Hitler and the rise of the U. S. and the U. S. S.
R. as the two dominant superpowers. The rivalry between these two
countries led the U. S. to implement a number of educational exchange
programs for students from the newly independent Muslim states of
Asia and Africa. These cultural programs of the U. S. government,
together with the official policies of the individual Muslim countries to
send students here, led to a dramatic increase in the Muslim student
population in the U. S. This increase in the student population and the
tension that soon developed between the Americanized Arab-Muslims
and their visiting cousins on American campuses, particularly in the
midwest—where there was a heavy concentration of descendants of
earlier immigrants—led to the creation of Muslim student organizations.[10] The Muslim Student Association (M. S. A) developed out of this

situation and its founding fathers consisted of several students who objected to the brand of Islam which was identified with the host community of Americanized Muslims.

The young M. S. A. leadership, determined to deal with the challenges from both the dangers of "Americanized Islam" and heretical brands of Islam of the NOI and Ahmadiyya varieties, established these chapters, seeing their task as that of Muslims who found themselves in a strange environment where their brief sojourn as seekers of knowledge demanded certain sacrifices. These Muslim students, it should be stressed, were not originally interested in a large scale institutionalization drive.

This original attitude towards the American environment changed as the institutional competition between the M. S. A. and the home-grown Arab-Muslim organizations became intense. With a large pool of students from different parts of the Muslim world to recruit from, the M. S. A. soon found itself a national organization with many chapters across the U. S. and Canada. These chapters would gradually serve as the nuclei of an emerging professional class of Muslims. Such a phenomenon has been most evident in big urban areas where the Muslim students have made the most successful transition from student life to professional life.[11] The present Muslim national organizations bear the fingerprints of the first and second generations of Muslim and their origins must be traced back to the first generations of the Muslim Student Association. To examine the roots of some of the other organizations and institutions now present in American Muslim Society, we must look at the histories of the Nation of Islam, the Ahmadiyya Movement, the various Sufi groups and the network of Arab Muslim organizations grouped under the Federation of Islamic Associations (FIA).[12]

The transformation of the NOI instituted by Imam Warith Deen Muhammad, the son and successor of the late Honorable Elijah Muhammad, has significance for Muslim efforts at institution-building on two grounds. First of all, it brought the entire movement into the fold of orthodox Islam and made the facilities of this social movement available to many orthodox Muslims who previously were either unwelcome or too aggravated by Elijah's teachings to join the NOI members in developing their institutions. The second point relating to the transformation of the NOI is the fact that the new teachings of the Imam opened the movement to all Americans, regardless of race, and at the same time made it categorically clear that both the African-American Muslims under Imam Muhammad and the M. S. A. have a common responsibility to safeguard the Muslim identity through institutionalization. Although a concatenation of circumstances going back to the 1930s led to the present division of labor between immigrants and native-born Americans, events of the late 1970s and early 1980s seem to suggest new ways of building bridges between the two communities.

Various obstacles stood in the way of Muslim missionaries (dais) with regards to Muslim institution-building and as a result we must note that three different types of persons are involved in this task. The first, are the custodians of the M. S. A. heritage, mainly professionals seeking social security and a sense of stability and continuity in the work of their national organizations, the Islamic Society of North America, ISNA, along with the local mosques or Islamic centers affiliated to it. The second type of institution-builder was the African-American Muslim whose previous rejection of the NOI's brand of Islam, led him to a variety of Islam designed to meet his sociological and psychological needs and conditions in America. As aforementioned, the African-Americans in the old NOI who followed Imam Warith Deen Muhammad in 1975, are described as the founders of the Islamic institutions which embody the Imam's serious attempt to foster simultaneously Islamism and Americanism within the society as a whole. While taking note of such institutional developments, one must also point to the fact that, up until the successful transformation of the NOI into a veritable orthodox Muslim organization, there existed several other small orthodox Muslim groups in African-American society. Many of these Muslims, in their own way, tried hard to build institutions for the maintenance of the Islamic identity in the U. S. Mention should be made of Shaykh al-Hajj Daud Faisal (1891-1980), founder of the Islamic Mission of America in 1928, in Brooklyn, New York; of the leaders of the Islamic Party of North America; of leaders of the Islamic Brotherhood, Inc. in New York, which once published the Western Sunrise; the leaders of the Hanafi Movement, and the various leaders of mosques and centers where the light of Islamic orthodoxy flickered in those bitter years.[13]

In examining the role and contributions of the Arab-American Muslims in the creation and maintenance of Islamic institutions in the U. S., we must again remind ourselves that these Muslims embarked

upon this delicate task of institution building in search of self-preser-
vation and on a quest for cultural and religious continuity. A second or
third generation immigrant Muslim is separated from the core of his
own culture and religion by both time and space. These factors cause
him to see in his Muslim institutions and organizations an embodiment
of his desire to remain Muslim and of his will to reconcile this Muslim
identity with his American identity. It is his intention to accomplish this
as effectively and as successfully as his American Christian and Jewish
counterparts. But while working to make his own dream come true, this
Americanized Muslim neighbor, who too is laboring to construct an
Islamic identity and the structures that would give it meaning, and the
non-immigrant student whose Islamic missionary efforts could either be
remembered later on as those of a transient worker of Islam in the U. S.
or the first installment of service given by a former M. S. A. member
who has graduated into the ranks of the emerging Muslim professionals in the U. S.

THE CHALLENGE TO BUILD MUSLIM ECONOMIC STRUCTURES

In looking at the points of convergence and divergence within the
Muslim community, one finds that Muslim economic activity in the U.
S. was a problem for some leaders. Various problems exist, such as
Muslim attitudes towards interest (*riba*) as well as the question of ownership of property and the need to remain faithful to the Islamic precepts which are likely to be subverted by Muslim involvement with the
rules and practices of capitalist materialism. There is also the problem
of trading in forbidden (*haram*) merchandise, because goods like alco-
hol and pork are considered off-limits to Muslims. With these economic limitations in terms of activities within American society, strict orthodox Muslims are mostly condemned to lead a marginal existence in the
current American social system.

The American dream and the economic system which keeps this
dream alive, allows for several points of convergence and divergence
within the Muslim community to be identified and analyzed. Three
areas of mutual interest to the entire Muslim community in the U. S. fall
under the category of points of convergence. First, is the collective
desire of Muslims to survive as individuals, as families and as a community. For this and related reasons, they are willing to participate in

various ways in the American economy. These differential degrees of involvement with the American economy are demonstrated through the activities of the old Nation of Islam, the Darul Islam Movement, the Islamic Party of North America, the Ansarullah, the Hanafi and the ultra-orthodox Muslim organizations located in American cities. However, regardless of their differential attitudes toward the American economy, all of these groups are considered participants in the American economy and it is here that these African-American groups join their immigrant brothers in the game of economic survival within the U. S.

The second area of mutual interest is in the selling of Muslim products or merchandise useful to Muslims. Following the same path of other immigrants, Muslims found that the creation of their own businesses was the best avenue toward self-protection and toward the reduction of cultural trauma caused by the encounter with American society. Again, evidence supporting this point of convergence of the foreign-born Muslims and their native brethren can be gleaned from the number and types of businesses established by these two subgroups within the Muslim community. The creation of these business opportunities have provided all of these Muslim groups opportunities to assert themselves and to demonstrate their independence from the power of hiring and firing of the popular culture. As testimony to this success, students of American business history generally assert that the greater majority of small businesses are owned by foreign-born Americans and immigrants.[14]

In light of this understanding, one can now argue that the convergence of interest between the immigrant Muslims and their native-American co-religionists lies not only in the economic survival of their community, but also in the establishment of small businesses which strengthen them individually as well as collectively. Both the immigrants and the local Muslim Americans, see the various opportunities, but they do differ widely in their perceptions of and attitude toward the American economic system.

The third point of convergence between the immigrants and native-born American Muslims is the common interest in increasing the Muslim cultural presence in American society. This interest is inextricably linked to the economic question. By asserting their cultural presence,

Muslims hope to win over non-Muslim entrepreneurs to make conces-sions to their community by not trampling upon their sensitivities. This attitude is not limited to American Muslims. It is being developed in all countries where Muslims constitute a minority. But, while conceding to this development in the Muslim community, it cannot be ignored that Muslim small business owners would rather not have competition from other non-Muslim businesses. Such rivals, if allowed or convinced to extend their tentacles into the Muslim community, could reduce the independence of Muslim businessmen who are specialized in providing services to their fellow Muslims. These "neighborhood stores," in areas where Muslims are numerous, are definitely appreciated by the com-munity, although only a few Muslims might entertain the illusion that such businesses protect the Muslim from the economic penetration of the capitalist market.

When we look at the points of divergence, we find that the problem of interest in financial transactions remains the great divide between the rigidly orthodox Muslims and their counterparts who are willing to make adjustments to American society. Although it is dangerous to gen-eralize about Muslims all over the United States of America, one can argue that most of the practicing immigrant Muslims from the old world and a sizable number of strict orthodox African-American Muslims view interest (*riba*) with suspicion. Differing from their more accommodating brethren in two ways, these Muslims disagree on whether to participate actively in the U. S. economy and to take or pay interest. There is also a discrepancy in their perceptions of the American dream. The strictly orthodox do not define the American dream exclusively in terms of the ownership of creature comforts and of material things considered as status symbols in the larger society. The dream, if it is given any significant place in the strictly orthodox society, is a symbolic encapsulation of divine blessings (*baraka*) bestowed upon American society and its inhabitants by a generous Allah who grants this favor as a trial.

The accommodationist Muslim embraces the American dream without hesitation. Like his Christian or Jewish neighbors who adjust their religions to face the challenges of the secularization of society, the accommodationist maintains his commitment to his faith while making minor concessions which would be considered unacceptable by more rigidly orthodox co-religionists. The accommodationist views his presence in American-society as both an opportunity and a test from the Almighty. Unlike his orthodox co-religionists, he sees his rendezvous with the American dream as a grand opportunity to better himself and his family, and to demonstrate to the larger society that American Muslims do belong no matter what the religious bigot of the Muslim fanatic thinks of his relationship with the American dream.

In applying the categories developed earlier in our interpretation of the identity question among Muslims in the U. S.—particularly among African-Americans—we find that attitudes toward and opinions about the American economy and the American dream tend to be defined by how one fits in that spectrum of self-definition. Among the assimilationists who embrace Islam as a total way of life, a negative perception of and attitude toward the U. S. economy tends to develop. This ideological position is brought about by the convert's dissatisfaction with American society and by his perception and belief that much of what goes on around him is forbidden (*haram*) and un-Islamic. This type of convert joins the bandwagon of the Muslim faithfuls who seek alternatives to life with usurious interest (*riba*) in the United States of America.[15] There are also the Americans who embrace Islam and are willing to assimilate themselves into Islamic culture while still recognizing their ethnic origins. African-Americans and Latinos of this type embrace the American dream, seeing no serious conflict between it and their religion and they also do not shy away from participation in the U. S. economy. This second type, though more adaptive than the first type, is slightly different from the third in that the latter is more open and willing to Americanize his Islamic culture.

Opposed to the aforementioned types are the simulationists, previously described as Elijahian. Concerned with the maintenance of a separate identity apart from the larger community, the simulationists and the rigidly orthodox Muslims both share the attitude of rejection or isolation from mainstream society. Though the simulationists may, in the realm of theological purity, be dismissed as heretical or heterodox, in the realm of economic life and activity they share the same attitude towards the corporate economic system as the rigidly orthodox Muslims. Both groups agree that any deep and abiding interaction with the larger economic system erodes and undermines the pillars of their independent existence and identity; hence the attempts to promote economic independence through the creation of economic and business networks. The old NOI solved the economic problem through their quest for a separate state, resulting in the greatest success story of a simulationist drive when it was reported to have $75 million in assets at the time of its spiritual leader's death.

THE CHALLENGE TO PARTICIPATE IN AMERICAN POLITICAL LIFE

The historical record of Muslims in U. S. society shows that attitudes toward American politics are defined by the manner in which the Muslims see themselves in the society. The same divergent attitudes which we have seen with regard to the economy are also manifest in the political arena where the accommodationists have shown no hesitation to participate. For example, during the Second World War, when those followers of Elijah Muhammad and the followers of Sunni Muslim leader Shaykh al-Hajj Daud Faisal of Brooklyn, New York, claimed that their religion of Islam prohibited them from fighting with the U. S. military, American Muslims from the Middle East and southern and east Europe disagreed and signed up for the war zones, later collecting medals of valor. The followers of Shaykh Daoud joined the military in the late 1950's and 1960's.[16]

The African-American Muslims opposed the war because they felt that they were being used as cannon fodder by European and American Christians to settle their own scores. The Nation of Islam changed in the 1970's when Imam Warith Deen Muhammad assumed the role of its leader. Among the many changes which he ushered into this African-American group was the redefinition of attitudes toward America and her military establishment. Unlike his father, who authored the book *The Fall of America*, Imam Muhammad urged his followers to accept their American as well as their Islamic identity. According to the previous definitions, Imam Muhammad moves his father's organization from the simulationist to the assimilationist position. This is to say, he transformed his father's movement into a body of men and women who take pride in their American citizenship and remain steadfast in their practice of Islam in American society. Substantively, Imam Muhammad demolished the "idol of the tribe" by telling his followers that race should no longer determine membership, that they were part of the Muslim and human worlds, and that their responsibility was to Allah who brought them to this life. Related to these points of the Imam was his teaching that Muslims should participate in American politics. His reconstituted organization known as the World Community of Islam in the West and the American Muslim Mission, was later disbanded and authority was transferred to the local mosques. But before he effected this radical transformation of the old Nation of Islam, the Imam managed to plant the seeds of political participation among his flock around the country. As a result of his policy changes Muslims have now made some serious efforts to engage in political life in the U. S. with organizations such as the Muslim Political Action Committee in Greater Washington, D. C., which has received recognition from D. C. Mayor Marion Barry to the point where the Mayor, in his victory speech, listed Muslims after Christians and Jews as supporters of his successful campaign. Similar efforts have been made elsewhere in the country. In fact, the mosques of the American Muslim Mission have created a platform for political education of Muslims interested in politics, conferences dealing with political issues have been held in different locations throughout the country and one might be tempted to say that these meetings have played an important part in the political education and eventual mass participation of Muslims in American political life.

This transformation of the old American Muslim Mission into a vast networks of autonomous mosques around the country has encouraged local Muslims of African-American origin to partake in a variety of activities in their community. On the political front, these Muslims have seized the opportunity to seek positions in secular organizations which were previously avoided due to their integrationist approach toward American society. As a result of these changes in attitudes and perceptions, many Afro-American Muslims with political ambitions no longer hesitate to seek elective office within the American political system. Though the number of Muslim politicians within the larger Black community is negligible, there is reason to believe that, as the attitude change becomes more and more deeply rooted in Muslim African-America and in the larger Muslim community, chances are a few American politicians with Muslim names will begin to make the roster of U. S. elected officials.

But while the orthodox and not so orthodox African-American Muslims avoided politics in the U. S. because of their perception of and attitudes toward white society and its controlling establishment, the immigrant Muslims of the first, second and third generations reacted to the politics of the society differently due to an entirely different set of motives and reasons. Coming from countries where little or no democracy prevailed, most of the immigrant Muslims remained apathetic about politics in the U. S. However, this attitude changed significantly in the second generation of Muslims because of their greater assimilation into American culture and their greater identification with "the land of the free and the home of the brave." This new sense of patriotism, when skillfully tapped by urban or rural politicians in the midwestern and northeastern parts of the country, led to a greater politicization of these Muslims. But, even though these individuals were Muslims in their names and their identities within their local communities, the politicians who sought their votes appealed to them as American voters of a particular ethnic background. This is a crucial point to note, because up until the late 1970's, American Muslims did not organize or mobilize themselves as a political force within the American universe of political lobbies.

The earliest efforts of Muslims to seek recognition from the political leadership of this country, came from the leaders of the Federation of Islamic Association (FIA). Composed primarily of descendants of middle eastern Arabs, the FIA made some efforts to register the Muslim presence by appealing to President Eisenhower to allow Muslim members of the armed forces to have the letter I as their dog tag. They argued that the Christians had crosses and the Jews had Stars of David, therefore, in the name of social justice and of religious pluralism, the Muslims should be permitted to have the letter I. Abdullah Ingram, a World War Two veteran, was able to convince the U .S. authorities on this point and as a result, Muslims now have the letter I as their badge of religious identification in the multi-religious U. S. military.[17]

In analyzing the question of Muslim involvement in U. S. politics, and the divergent positions taken by the numerous groups within the community, one must also note the changes in the Muslim population that resulted from the immigration of a large number of highly educated Muslims from various parts of the Muslim world, specifically from the Middle East and South East Asia. This influx of new and better educated Muslims has had political implications which are yet to be properly understood. Though time and space do not allow us to dwell on these implications, we can still identify the factors responsible for the change in attitude toward the American political process. The first factor to consider is the emergence of the national Muslim organizations that were committed to the assertion of a Muslim American identity. Unlike the F. I. A. which has been perceived in Muslim circles, as an organization catering to descendants of Arab Muslims from Lebanon and the Fertile Crescent, the new organizations, such as the Islamic Society of North America (ISNA), are led and financed by immigrant Muslims. They project their organizations as continental societies for all Muslims. Though this image may be challenged by others in the community, the fact remains that ISNA with all its weaknesses and short-comings still serves as one of the few Muslim organizations which is connected to thousands of Muslims around the country. Over the last five years, due to a growth of self-confidence and an increase in anti-Muslim harassments and attacks in the media and in the larger U. S. community, some members of the ISNA leadership have begun to seri-ously consider the political option. This political option calls for greater and more active Muslim Political Action Committee. In an issue of the *Islamic Horizons* (November, 1987), one Nahid Khan writes:

> After years of watching both local and national pol-
> iticking from the sidelines, Muslims are beginning to realize
> that it's time for the community to make its entrance into the
> political arena. In moving in this direction, the Islamic
> Society of North America (ISNA) has recently filed with the
> Federal Election Commission to form a Political Action
> Committee (PAC) and is now awaiting approval, according to
> the ISNA Secretary General Iqbal Unus.[18]

Khan adds that the decision of ISNA is part of "a scant group of Muslim communities and organizations who have already started to test the political waters."[19] He also identified the United Muslims of America of California, the Texas-based All-American Muslim Political Action Committee (AAMPAC) and the League of Muslim Voters in Chicago as a part of this group. The decision to engage in political activ-ities in North America has been debated within ISNA since the late 1970's. The idea won majority support in 1986 when the consultative body (*Majlis al-shura*) of ISNA, decided to lobby politically to call on all Muslims to become more involved in the American and Canadian polit-ical processes.

The political option is now shared by both the followers of Imam

Warith Deen Muhammad and the members of the Islamic Society of North America. These two organizations represent a significant portion of the Muslim community and their involvement in the American political process could give greater visibility to Muslims and issues of interest to them.

CONCLUSIONS

The identity question is central to the Muslim presence in the U. S. The American Muslim can only maintain his identity by holding steadfastly on to the rope of unity of God (*tawhid*). This is definitely not an easy task, because there are numerous forces at work which are likely to make life difficult. Yet, as we have shown, the Islamic identity is now a reality, the manner in which it is defined and projected varies from Muslim to Muslim. We have already identified the divergent attitudes towards U. S. society among American Muslims. In this conclusion we can say that although Muslims differ in some of the burning issues of American society their sense of unity is evident in their common faith in *tawhid*, in their collective practice of Muslim rituals and in the expression of solidarity on matters affecting all Muslims living in the U. S. To put this another way, one could say that, though divergence exists in the realm of perceptions of and attitudes toward American society, convergence exists in the realm of rituals and fellow feelings towards one's own co-religionists. This state of affairs is certainly not peculiar to Muslims. It is evident in other religious communities living within the U. S.

In this essay, one arrives at another conclusion: that institution-building among Muslims has been slow. This was largely due to the type of immigrant Muslim who came to America and the slow conversion pace of native-born Americans who were intellectually and socially equipped to take the leadership in this process. It should be noted that these immigrants who had the capacity to found Muslim institutions were primarily interested in making money in the shortest amount of time in order to return to their respective countries. In addition, in the late nineteenth and early twentieth century, Muslims were defensive with regards to their relationship with the western countries and Muslim immigrants were not psychologically prepared to settle permanently outside of Darul Islam.

The third conclusion is the idea that Muslim economic structures are beginning to emerge and their success depends on the availability of capital within the Muslim community and on the attitudes of Muslim business people towards the American capitalist system. The divergent attitudes identified in our classification of different definitions of the Muslim identity in the U. S. will significantly effect on the future role of Muslims in the U. S. economy. As stated above, the assimilationist Muslims would fare as well as the assimilationist members of other religious traditions operating within the U. S. economy, developing intellectual justifications for dealing with banks that charge interest and with home-building companies that include interest in their mortgage rates. The simulationists, on the other hand, in the coming years will create economic structures that are faithful to Islamic economics, reassuring those who believe in God and the Traditions (*sunna*) of Prophet Muhammad.

The fourth conclusion is that the rise in Muslim self-confidence and the increase in the number of Muslims in the country is bound to lead the assimilationist Muslim to participate more and more within the American political system. Related to this is the fact that the trends in interreligious relations in the U. S. and the Muslim world could affect not only the image of the Muslim in the U. S., but also his perception of self in American society. For this reason, we now conclude that the future of Muslim survival in U. S. society is inextricably linked to the future of religious pluralism in this country. Any radical alteration in the pattern of religious pluralism in U. S. society could threaten not only Muslim Americans but all other minorities who are targeted for discrimination. If the present and the recent past are any sort of guide to the future, then we can here conclude that Islam as a minority religion has a promising future and Muslims, in the coming years, will be as well adjusted as any other religious minority. Their religion will join Christianity and Judaism as the third branch of the Abrahamic tradition, and for this reason, Will Herberg's statement on American religion will be amended to say that being American means that one may be a member of the Christian, Jewish, Muslim or any of the other religious traditions in American society.

NOTES TO 5

CONVERGENCE AND DIVERGENCE IN AN EMERGENT
COMMUNITY: A STUDY OF CHALLENGES FACING U. S.
MUSLIMS

1 For some insights on the racial situation in the United States before enforced desegregation became the law of the land, see Gunner Myrdal's book *An America Dilemma* (Anniv. Edition, New York: Harper and Row, 1964).

2 See Sulayman S. Nyang's editorial in the *American Journal of Islamic Studies* Vol. 1, No. 1.

3 Included in this category are groups like The Ansarullah; The Islamic Party of North America; The Islamic Brotherhood, Inc.,of New York; The Darul Islam Movement, and the Institute of Islamic Involvement in Winston-Salem, North Carolina. For details on their views of Islam in America, read the numerous publications of the Ansars, the back issues of *al-Islam, The Western Sunrise*, the *Jihadul Akbar*, and *Vision*.

4 Although there is no agreement on the number of Muslims in the United States of America, a widely cited figure is three million. For latest attempts at tabulations see Yvonne Haddad *Islamic Values in the United States: A Comparative Study* (New York:Oxford University Press, 1987). Arif Ghayur, "Muslims in the United States: Settlers and Visitors," Annals ASPSS, 454 (March, 1981).

5 For some treatment of the history of the Nation of Islam in the United States, see C. Eric Lincoln, *The Black Muslim in America* (Boston: Beacon Press, 1961); E.U. Essien-Udom, *Black Nationalism* (New York: Dell Publishing Co., Inc., 1962). For details on the transformation of the Nation of Islam, see Clifton E. Marsh, *From Black Muslims to Muslim* (Metuchen, New Jersey: The Scarecrow Press Inc., 1984); Akbar Muhammad, "Muslims in the United States: An Overview of Organizations, Doctrines and Problems"; In *The Islamic Impact*, Yvonne Haddad, Byron Haines and Ellison Findly, eds. (Syracuse: Syracuse University Press, 1984), pp. 195-218.

6 See the chronology of major historical events for Muslim America in Yvonne Haddad, *A Century of Islam in America*. Occasional paper No. 4 (Washington, D. C.: American Institute of Islamic Affairs, 1986), p. 10.

7 See Sulayman S. Nyang, "Growth of Islam in America," The Saudi Gazette, October 19, 1983.

8 Richard B. Turner, "The Ahmadiyya Movement in Islam in America," unpublished paper, p. 3.

9 Abdo El-Kholy, *The Arab Moslem in America* (New Haven, Connecticut: College and University Press, 1966), p.48.

10 For more information on the MSA and its activities, see back issues of *al-Ittihad* and *Islamic Horizons*.

11 See Sulayman S. Nyang and Mumtaz Ahmad, "The Muslim Intellectual Emigre in the United States," *Islamic Culture*, IX (1985), 277-90.

12 See Lincoln, *op. cit.*; Turner, *op. cit.*; El-Kholy, *op. cit.*.

13 For details on the activities of these Muslim groups in the African-American community, see Sulayman S. Nyang and Robert J. Cummings, *Islam in the United States* (forthcoming), especially chapter on "Islam and the Black Experience in the USA."

14 See Sulayman S. Nyang's "Muslim Minority Business Enterprise in the United States," *The Search*, Vol. 3, No.2 (Spring, 1982).

15 The Ansarullah Movement and members of ultra-conservative Muslim groups fall under this category. Such persons usually do not like the idea of paying interest on home mortgages,interest on credit cards and on other usury (*riba*) activities.

16 Interviews with Bedria Saunders, Bilal Abdul Rahman and his wife Rakiya in Brooklyn, New York (Spring, 1982).

17 Abdo El-Kholy, quoting an F. I. A. document, maintains that Muslims in the U. S. army were relegated to the residual X category. See his *Arab Moslems in the America*, p. 46.

18 See *Islamic Horizons* (November, 1987), p.13.

19 *Ibid.*

6

THE PROPHET MUHAMMAD, ISLAM AND THE WEST

A few decades ago it was unthinkable for an American intellectual or a Muslim intellectual living in the heartland of Daral Islam to imagine Muslim ministries in the heartland of the West. Today this is a reality that no one can deny. What happened over the last four decades since World War II? How have developments in migration, in telecommunications and in the televillagization of the world changed the nature of the relationship between Muslims and the West? How can interested parties within Daral Islam build effective bridges of communication with westerners to enhance understanding and avoid conflict? What can Muslims in the West do to open lines of communication with various groups in Western societies, now that their destinies are inextricably linked to those of non-Muslims in the West? These and other related questions are the focus of this essay. Before entering into a discussion of each question in detail, one must establish what exactly is meant by the terms "Islam" and "the West."

ON THE DEFINITION OF TERMS: ISLAM AND THE WEST

Islam in this paper is used to encompass the body of beliefs accepted by Muslims who see themselves as *ahl al-sunna* (faithful adherents to beliefs and practices revealed to the Prophet Muhammad in the Quran and captured for posterity in such books of Hadith and *sunna* as al-Bukhari, Muslim Tirmidhi, etc.). This community, known as *al-ummah* to Muslims, is both metahistorical and international; this is to say, it transcends time and space and it embraces all peoples, languages and cultures of the world. For this and other related reasons, the definition of Islam has two dimensions. At one level, it refers to the beliefs and practices of the religion, and, at another level, it alludes to the community of believers who embody in their lives the teachings of Islam. Hence, Islam refers to both a community and a belief system.

The term West is also used to denote both a community and the diverse beliefs lumped together in its name. Unlike the term Islam, the term "West" is a secular-cum-religious concept. That is to say, it embraces a peculiar set of historical experiences which have pitted secular forces against religion. As a result, the term "West" often leads to misunderstanding and miscommunication because those who do the comparing and contrasting often forget that the anti-clericalism of Western history is unknown to Islam. The centrality of what Westerners called secular humanism in both human perception and engagement of life is a recent phenomenon for Muslims, largely a result of the colonial and post-colonial experience. In light of this fact, it is important for Muslims to remember that the term "West" is now primarily a civilizational term that describes a culture whose predominance in human society and world history is pegged in a descending order on a military, economic, cultural and political complex. As a result of this multidimensional hegemony in human affairs, those who compare Islam and the West often commit the error of looking at Islam as a religion and the West as a civilization. To do justice to Islam one must look at it as a civilization also, with its own peculiar characteristics.

After spelling out these differences and pointing to the risks of faulty comparisons, one should also remember that the civilizational reach of the West is now global. Nevertheless, for the sake of this analysis one can safely say that western civilization consists of the Catholic and Protestant countries of western Europe and the diasporic states created by the descendants of Europeans and other human groups in North America, Australia and New Zealand. This is the cultural West, whose identity has been defined up to the Age of Discovery by a European land-base, by white skin color, by adherence to Christianity, and by belonging to what linguists call an Indo-European language family. This definition of Westerners went through some changes over the last five hundred years because of the migration of large numbers of peoples who were historically non-Christian, non-white and linguistically non-Indo-European into the original homelands of westerners. The first outsiders in the days of religious and "racial" exclusiveness were the Jews and Slavs from southern and central Europe respectively. The Jews who were part of the Islamic civilization in the Middle East and on the Iberian Peninsula were forced out of Spain, along with Muslims, after the fall of Granada and the institution of the Inquisition from 1492 onward. The dispersal of Jews to places like Holland, England and Eastern Europe would lead later to the widening of the cultural zone of inter-religious co-existence and the potential acceptance and coalescence of Jews as a part of the western identity. This was not to happen until the 19th century, when Napoleon Bonaparte launched what Jewish scholars call the Emancipation. It was not until then that western Christians came to accept Jews as real westerners. Similarly, one could say that the racial exclusiveness of the western self-definition denied the humanity of the African until the American post-bellum constitutional amendments elevated him from three-fifths of a man to the more dignified status of legal manhood. This legal equality remained at the level of theory until the Supreme Court ruling on the age-old separate but equal doctrine was reversed in the now famous Brown vs. the Board of Education in Topeka, Kansas. It was at this time that the Civil Rights Movement made it categorically clear that America must live up to the ideals contained in the Declaration of Independence.

To return to the issue of the expanding definition of who is a westerner, it is interesting to note that, on both the western mainland and in the diasporic extensions, the 19th century was a period of adjustment. The influx of refugees and immigrants from eastern Europe and Asia led to racist policies. In the United States one read about the "yellow peril," fear of the "yellow races," and the enactment of the Chinese Exclusion Act of the 1890's. In Australia, the legal response was the adoption of a white-only immigration policy.

These exclusionary acts of western mainlanders and diasporans would be changed by war and massive relocations of peoples from war zones. Related to but separate from these developments are the unintended consequences of the Cold War. Owing to the top priority of winning the Cold War, strategists in the West revised their immigration laws to welcome refugees from Soviet and Communist oppression. A similar motivation led to the institutionalization of the process of educating non-westerners in western schools and universities. This was instituted as a way to recruit and train potential cold warriors among Africans,

Asians and Latin Americans. Many of these potential allies either remained in the West after their studies or were driven back to the West by political circumstances beyond their control in their countries of origin.

A BRIEF HISTORY OF MUSLIM IMMIGRATION TO THE USA

Anyone looking at the relationship between the West and the Muslim world must take into account the historical realities which shape the relationship. As a result of the changes described above, and owing to the unintended consequences of the Cold War, Muslims, Hindus, Buddhists, Bahais and a host of strange and unknown religious, cultural and linguistic groupings are now living on both the western mainland and in the diasporic West. Each of these groups are now western in identity, whether the host society likes it or not. Indeed history, biology and human psychology have always conspired to play tricks on the builders of civilizations. Western Civilization as embodied in North America has expanded its range of acceptance to embrace, however grudgingly, certain elements of Judaism. The African-American identity is now also a part of the American identity, and racism is no longer overtly sanctioned by United States courts.

It is indeed against this background that one can identify the issues facing Muslims and their religion in the West. It is also in such a large context that one can look at the life and example of the Prophet Muhammad. Those of us engaged in a lifetime dialogue with non-Muslim neighbors and fellow citizens can enrich knowledge of ourselves and of our community by increasing our database with items from the life and times of the Prophet.

CHALLENGES FACING ISLAM IN THE WEST

In discussing the relationship between Islam and the West, one must take into account the challenges facing Muslims and their religion in the West. The first challenge is the question of identity. Muslims in the West in general, and in North America in particular, all agree that they share a common belief in the Quran and *sunna*. However, traditional sectarian (*madhabian* and *tariqian*) differences have lingered on in America, and added to these are peculiarly American developments which have made the definition and identification of the cultural parameters of

Islam difficult to understand within the context of the dominant majority society. Here one must look at to two developments in North America
since the beginning of this century.

The emergence and proliferation of divisionist groups has made it
difficult for the average North American to distinguish between the
Islamic and the Islamized. As a result of this confusion, many Americans
now confuse the larger Muslim community with marginal groups
whose activities are clear deviations from the inheritance of the Prophet
and the Quran. Owing to this confusion about the Muslim community,
the message of the Prophet Muhammad is undermined not only by the
excesses of orientalism but also by what I have called Popcorn Sufism
and MacWorld Islamism. These two concepts were created to describe
two phenomena which are evident in the American religious landscape
today.

Popcorn Sufis are individuals who claim a Sufi mystical tradition
which leads them to indulge in rituals without any connection to the five
pillars of Islam. To borrow a term from Stephen Carter's new book, *A
Culture of Disbelief*, Popcorn Sufis are Americans who exercise their
first amendment rights to believe in a religious practice which is strictly a hobby. Unlike orthodox Sufis, such as Imam al-Ghazzali and countless others in Muslim history, western New Age varieties do not believe
in the religion of Allah and do not give any evidence of following the
sunna of the Prophet.

The twin of Popcorn Sufism is MacWorld Islamism. This phenomenon is purely an American invention. It has manifested itself historically in groups that appropriated certain elements of Islam into their belief
system and rituals. Because of their likeness to and simulation of things
Islamic, most North Americans have great difficulty in separating true
Islam from these distortions. North Americans also fail to understand
Islam as a religion, a culture, a community and a civilization. Because
of the polarity of race, skin color, national origin and religion, which
have served as effective demarcation lines in their definition of self,
these North Americans do not have any meaningful understanding of
their Muslim neighbors. The teachings and life examples of the Prophet
Muhammad can only be made known to non-Muslims in society
through effective, open and unapologetic missionary work. Americans
and other westerners must learn that there are fellow citizens who are
mirror opposites of the images supplied by orientalist literature on one

hand, and by Popcorn Sufis and MacWorld Islamized groups on the other. Until then, the identity and image of Muslims in the United States will remain distorted in the larger mirror of American and Canadian society.

Directly linked to the Muslim image in the American mirror is the question of the Muslim's definition and understanding of his or her newly acquired citizenship in Western (North American) society. In order for Muslims to fight successfully the negative images their enemies have created and perpetrated, three things must be done. First of all, Muslims must assert and affirm their membership in the American community. By doing this the Muslim reassures doubting non-Muslims that he or she is not a marginal actor in American civilization whose only interest is either to live undisturbed on the Islamic ghetto margins or to seize control of the civilization altogether. Neither of these two alternatives are acceptable to Muslims who see the life and example of the Prophet Muhammad as a guidebook to life at all times.

The first alternative is a life which Meccans would have liked Prophet Muhammad to adopt in the early years of Islam. The Prophet did not confine himself to mount Hira; rather, he climbed down and went to the Kabah and confronted the deniers of *tawhid* (unity of God) and the distorters of Allah's message who simulated *tawhid* at one level but undermined it at others. The Prophet Muhammad did not confine himself to the comforting embrace of his clan quarters; he ventured out to Taif where his enemies showed their disbelief and cruelty by setting their ferocious dogs and their local urchins on him. These examples from the *sirah* of the Prophet serve as reminders to Muslims, especially to those in the Black community, who have created a comfort zone called Islam against what is usually dismissed off-handedly as non-believing America. Such attitudes have not been and are not likely to help in the quest for change in the image of Muslims. Acting like the proverbial ostrich only provides a false sense of security while the enemies and detractors of Islam capture the political and moral high ground.

Similarly, those who refuse to be assimilated into North American society do nothing to correct American misconceptions. People who employ this tactic are the opposite of Muslims who are comfortable with their self-imposed ghettoized lifestyles on the margins of society. These Muslims are part of what I have described elsewhere as the simulationists, who see no need to partake in the larger society because of its "corruption and its anti-Islamic way of life." Condemned as ignorant (*jahili*) and satanic, America stands accused in the eyes of these Muslims as ignorant and diabolical. Some extremists advocate a Medinite model and urge their fellow travellers to prepare for a revolutionary day when Allah's helpers will triumph. Such a way of thinking borders on messianism and millenarianism. Elements in the West with such an outlook on life are a minority, whose existence is facilitated both by their sense of alienation from the mainstream culture and by their sense of guilt wrapped in romantic rhetoric. The sense of guilt is stronger among immigrants, whereas among native-born North Americans, identification with messianism is largely occasioned by system-challenging feelings. Such feelings, wherever they exist, are almost always the result of rage and bitterness among America's violated minorities.

Another challenge facing Muslims is the quest for a place in the cultural landscape. Culture is a human enterprise that has three components, namely, a material base, a value base and an institutional base. Thus, in addition to the identity question, the question of cultural location becomes the second most important issue for Muslims. The quest for a cultural change in America means that Muslims must secure both a mental and a physical space that they can call their own in American society. For this to happen, they must make sure that institutions and structures are put in place to cater to their material needs in both general and specific ways. Their values should not be compromised to the point that Islam is no longer what it is supposed to mean to them. Their social, economic and spiritual agencies for social self-definition and self-reproduction should be effectively maintained through individual and group action.

Within the mental space of the Muslim community, a number of intellectual battles might rage, depending on the cultural diversity of the community, the political climate in the larger society and the economic circumstances of the Muslims. If the Muslim community is highly fragmented along sectarian, ethnic, linguistic, class and political ideological lines, then the process I call islandization will take place. Such a state of affairs will result in a proliferation of outwardly religious organizations which are ethnic outfits hiding behind Islamic masks. With organizations like these, the Muslim community becomes metaphorically a chain of cultural and ethnic islands, separated from each other by indices

which have nothing to do with Islam. Because of the absence of inte-
grative elements such as Islamic consciousness and social solidarity,
Muslim society could easily be manipulated by groups bent on prevent-
ing its successful assertion of a distinct religious identity within the
framework of American society.

Manipulators within the community have already been identified.
Those from outside can be either secularly or religiously motivated.
Secular fundamentalists are pathologically obsessed with Islam, and are
determined to hide behind the first amendment to rebuke, scandalize
and stigmatize Islam as one of the most fatal threats to the constitutional order in America. These people would be quite pleased to drive a
wedge between the races, ethno-linguistic groups, classes in Muslim
communities. They would also like to secularize the differences between
Muslims, and to attribute to Islam the causes of their problems.
Religious fundamentalists are better known as the religious right, whose
enlightened self-interest would be better served by identifying points of
convergence with the Muslims. Unfortunately, this group often takes an
antagonistic position toward Muslims, both out of fear and out of ideological hostility.

Due to the perceived and real opposition from both ends of the ideological spectrum in the United States, it is dangerous and unwise for
Muslims not to engage in dialogue with other members of American
society. It is only through dialogue and political action that Muslims can
define their individual and group interests. Taking full advantage of
their citizenship in North America and learning to join hands with other
forces shaping the society, Muslims could build up structures to satisfy
their group interests and to replicate in the form of public policy certain ideas that are in both the national interest and their own. For example, Muslims can over time convince both policy makers and the business elite of the need for official recognition of *id* holidays. Business
elites, who are mainly driven by profit motives, could be sufficiently
influenced by Muslim purchasing power to appreciate Muslim dietary
needs. An effective and conscientious community can certainly create
the conditions for a gradual, or even a rapid change in American attitude toward Muslims. This is an uphill battle and vigilance and hard
work should be key for Muslim leaders and those they lead.

Considering the diversity within the Muslim community, and taking
into account the high degree of literacy and technical competence

among Muslims, and especially among immigrants, Muslims in North America should organize themselves and make greater use of American technology to assert their identity and give assistance to Muslims in the old world. This challenge of technical and moral leadership by North American Muslims can only become a reality once four programs of action have been developed and implemented.

The first program must focus on the re-affirmation of a global Islamic consciousness through the use of technological facilities available to Muslims in the West. This global Islamic consciousness program could best be institutionalized through the celebration of Muslim unity and diversity on a date which is a holiday for most people in the West. Here the seven days between Christmas and New Year provide an opening for Muslims to share their faith with non-Muslims and to invite people from the Muslim World to sample products made by North American companies with Muslim interest. Such an annual festival celebrating the unity in diversity of the Muslim Community could open new doors of opportunity for Muslim businesses at home and abroad.

The second program which would help the North American Muslim to face the challenge of moral and technological leadership is the financing of first rate Muslim colleges in the United States and Canada by Muslim business leaders. By setting up credible and technologically and theologically well-grounded colleges for the education of Muslims in North America and beyond, Muslim business men and educators in North America would be able to gain greater attention in the Muslim World. It must be remembered that leadership in the Muslim World looks up to the West. Now that there are over five million highly trained Muslims in the West, it would be rational and realistic to expect greater involvement of North American Muslims in the transformation of Muslim societies.

The third program is the creation of Muslim NGOs (non-governmental organizations) in the West for the purpose of serving the needs of Muslims in North America and beyond. By creating social welfare organizations, Muslims on this side of the Atlantic Ocean may begin to implement the teachings and examples of the Prophet through direct community action. National newspapers and magazines have recently reported that certain Muslim organizations have embarked successfully on anti-drug campaigns in their localities. Their successes have on most occasions won them accolades, and rival religious groups have been sufficiently affected to duplicate such efforts in certain urban communities in the United States. By strengthening existing NGOs, and by developing a framework for closer cooperation and dissemination of ideas, North American Muslims might be able to give an American embodiment to the examples of the Prophet Muhammad. By carrying out such programs and by educating the uninformed American about the Islamic idea of alms (*zakat*) and charity (*sadaqa*), Muslims may well be able to create a new image of themselves and their communities.

The fourth program is the creation of new structures which are designed specifically to address the needs of second-and third-generation Muslims in North American society. In order for these generations of Muslims to survive the trauma of cultural adjustment in America, they must find a welcoming home away from home in the larger Muslim community. In our history we learn from the prophetic example of the mosque and its uses in socializing, educating, integrating and reassuring younger members of the community. Over the last fourteen hundred years the mosque has undergone several changes. In North America, new structures must be created to help reinforce the Islamic identity of younger generations and open channels of communication between older and younger Muslims. One program which might be helpful would be A Home-Away-From-Home Program. Such a program should create the opportunity for Muslims to deal with the generation gap, the native language deficit question, the potential conflicts of intergenerational contacts and the issues of value-environmental dissynchronization. For North American Muslims to deal effectively with such issues, a combination of scientific skills in the societal and behavioral sciences and an unreserved commitment to Muslim identity and community must be evident.

CONCLUSIONS

To conclude this analysis of the Prophet Muhammad, Islam and the West, the following points must be made:

(1) Islam is now a reality in North America, and both Muslims and their neighbors must make the necessary adjustments to arrive at a workable relationship in the years ahead;

(2) Extremist ideologies on both ends of the American political spectrum should be expected to make life difficult for Muslims if they

do not step forward and assert their citizenship strongly and unapologetically and defend their attendant right to contribute to and benefit from the American dream;

(3) The future of Muslims in North America depends on strategies and programs they design to strengthen global Islamic consciousness and Muslim technological ingenuity in North America and beyond;

(4) Examples from the life of the Prophet can be used effectively through social welfare organizations formed by North American Muslims. Muslim NGOs based in North America could educate Americans to appreciate Muslim ethics and social thought on a wide range of issues;

(5) The distinction between genuine Islamic groups and pseudo-islamized ones can only be made clear to non-Muslim Americans when Popcorn Sufis and MacWorld Islamism are seen for what they are. Such deviationist New Age groups can only be checked by vigilant and meticulous study and understanding of their programs and activities;

(6) Muslims of North America can maintain their distinct identity by taking their first amendment rights seriously and joining other forces shaping society all around them. Muslims in North America in particular, and the West in general, must be conservative enough not to bargain away their religion, but liberal enough to seize any political opportunity to form alliances with others whose interest can merge with theirs at a particular time and place. Muslims in North America must recognize the limitations of their minority status in this hemisphere, but in doing so, they must not chip away at the foundations of their radical monotheistic faith in order to belong and to be accepted. This would be too heavy a price to pay.

7

The Islamic Press in the United States of America

The birth of the Islamic Press in the United States of America dates back to the 19th and early 20th centuries. As pointed out in Sulayman Nyang's "Islam in the United States of America: A review of the Sources," published in both the April, 1981 issue of the Islamic Culture of India and in one of the 1981 issues of the *Journal of the Institute of Muslim Minority Affairs* in Jeddah, the literature on Islam and Muslims in the United States of America can be divided into three specific periods. The first is the colonization period. The second is the period starting from 1900 and ending in the 1950s and the third is the period since 1960. In this study of the Islamic Press in the United States, our focus is on the last two periods identified above.

During the late nineteenth and early twentieth century the number of Muslims in the United States was very small. Most, if not all immigrants were illiterate. This state of affairs had a noticeable effect on the development of an Islamic/Muslim Press in the country. The situation was destined to change with an unexpected development in the fortunes of the Islamic Movement of America. In the early 1890s, Mr. Alexander Russell Webb, an American diplomat, embraced Islam and decided to publicize its message around the country. His effort in this regard led to the founding of *The Muslim World*, the first Muslim periodical published in the United States. Published and edited by Webb, a white American who converted to Islam while serving as United States Consul in Manila, Philippines, this paper was destined to be the mother of the U. S. Islamic Press. *The Muslim World*, which was started in May, 1893, was a sixteen-page publication with various articles expounding upon and defending Islam in American society. Webb, whose biography is currently being written by Dr. Akbar Muhammad of the State University of New York at Binghamton, used his periodical to promote Islamic thought. Not only did he correct misconceptions about Islam and show the moral contrast between it and Christianity, but he also contemplated the establishment of a free library and reading room at 458 West 20th Street in New York city. He looked forward to the establishment of free lectures by Indian, Egyptian and Turkish promoters of missionary work in America.

These early efforts of Webb would not continue under an effectively institutionalized organization of Muslim men and women. Nevertheless, in retrospect one can say that Webb planted the seed of Islam and his efforts stirred some of the more enlightened Muslim immigrants to engage in missionary work. The International Muslim Union was formed in New York contemporaneously with Webb's group, but to date no extant copies of their publications have been found.

According to Beverly Mehdi, one hundred and two Arabic language newspapers and periodicals came into existence between 1898 and 1929. Obviously the mortality rate was very high for these publications and only a few survived and succeeded. Yet, in retrospect, one may share with Raouf Halaby the feeling expressed in his recent article in *The Syrian World*, one of the earliest Arab-American newspapers in America, that such output demonstrated "the Arabs' ingenious ability to adopt a western technology [geared solely to the use of the English alphabet] to his native Semitic Arab alphabet."

Out of these many Arabic newspapers the *al-Bayan* (The Statement) of the Syrian Druze Community provided the most direct reading facilities to Muslims. The others did carry news items about Muslims and the Islamic World, but *The Syrian World* was here the leader. According to Raouf Halaby, "[e]xamples of *The Syrian World*'s approach are seen in its treatment of religio-historical, ethnographic, and cultural themes of Christian, Druzi, and Islamic nature. It quoted sayings of the Prophet and Christ."

The decade of 1920s marks the arrival in Detroit of the prominent Sudano-Egyptian journalist, Duse Muhammad Ali. According to a recent paper by Ian Duffield of Edinburgh University, this newspaperman, who had already established a worldwide reputation as editor of the *African Times and Orient Review* in England, helped form an institutional namesake to his Central Islamic Society of London in Detroit. Though no extant publication has yet been found, it is quite conceivable that Duse Muhammad Ali and his fellow Muslims in the midwest published a newsletter to link different groups within the Muslim community there.

What is certain is the fact that by the early 1930s the Arab population and the Pakistani group called the Ahmadiyya began to publish literature on Islam. Though rejected as a member of the orthodox Islamic community since its inception in British India, the Ahmadiyya group managed to project an "Islamic image" for itself abroad, particularly in the United States. Beginning in the 1920s, when its first missionaries set sail for America, the Ahmadiyya started to publish *The Muslim Sunrise*. This periodical was expected to introduce the Ahmadi message to the American people. Mirza Ghulam Ahmad, who had a series of written exchanges with American religious leaders, including the controversial Christian-Zionist Joseph Dowie, felt that his *Muslim Sunrise* could save America from moral degeneration.

In addition to these efforts of the South Asian Muslims, there were also contributions to the growing Islamic press in America from the Arab Middle Eastern community. Arab Muslim migration to America dates back to the late 19th and early 20th centuries. Coming mainly from Palestine, the Levant and the Fertile Crescent, these Muslims mainly were drawn from the Fellahin class. Palestinian Muslim migration is a good example of this phenomenon.

At the turn of the 19th century, many Palestinian Arabs from the village of Ramallah migrated to Chicago and settled in furnished rooms in the neighborhood of 18th Street and Michigan Avenue. Attracted to the United States by tales of success reported by Armenians and Syrians, the first group took up peddling, working from door to door with such wares as oriental rugs, tablecloths, napkins, and so forth, which they carried in suitcases. By 1912 there were 150 Arab peddlers in Chicago, many of whom were Muslims.

Three factors were responsible for the early migration of Arab Muslims. The first is the political turmoil in the Ottoman Empire, which drove many Arab Christians out of the Middle East. Some Muslims, after much hesitation, likewise decided to come to the U. S. The second incentive for migration was the economic success stories of Arab immigrants already in the United States. Finally, many Arabs found the freedom and material lifestyle of America attractive and decided to stay in the U. S. permanently.

Some Arab papers warned about the dangers of marrying out of the Arab Islamic fold. On page three of the *al-Hayat* there were always features of decided interest to the readers. Invariably, the paper examined a contemporary or historical issue with the intention of drawing a political moral. From a careful analysis of some of the extant copies of the magazine, one can conclude that the Arabian Nights type of anecdote recitation thus persevered as a literary form in Chicago. The tenor of *al-Hayat* was one of a regenerated Islam. This approach to Muslim acculturation was a limited one, which differed greatly from that advanced at the time by another major Arabic newspaper, *al-Sameer*. Yet, in drawing this contrast, one should hasten to add that all Arabic newspapers operating in the United States in the late 1940s agreed on one point: the preservation of Arab Palestine.

Muslims were also a part of the waves of Albanians emigrating to the United States at that time. They settled in Massachusetts in the first half of the 20th century. According to a study on Albanians (1919), the more important settlements were located in the New England states, with the exception of Vermont, and in New York, Pennsylvania, Ohio, Michigan and Washington. Although some of them sailed directly to Boston, most of them disembarked at New York and traveled from there to New England, where they joined their relatives and friends and sought employment. In Albania they had been farmers, but they did not take up agriculture in the United States, since it required more capital than they possessed and also involved permanent settlement. They came to the U. S. alone, without their families, intending to save their money, return to Albania with the proceeds of their stay in America, and extend their goods and property there.

The jobs commonly taken by peasant immigrants were positions as unskilled laborers in textile mills, shoe factories, metal works, restaurants and hotels. Most Albanians settled in Boston and Worcester because of the opportunities for factory work in these places. A number of them migrated to Southbridge, where they worked in the factories of the American Optical Company. In New Bedford, hundreds of Albanians, mostly Muslims, were employed in textile mills, forming the largest Muslim-Albanian community in the state.

The Albanian workers lived in groups of ten to fifteen men in single flats called "*konak*," which were located in the slum areas of the cities. After World War I many Albanians went back to their country of origin and proceeded to marry and go into business and farming. Most of the Albanians who returned to their homeland were Muslims. On the other hand, those Muslims who "had established successful businesses stayed in America. Back in the United States, the Albanians revealed a profoundly changed attitude. Resolved to settle permanently, they now sought to fit themselves into their adopted country."

Muslim Albanians were part of the wave of ethnic Albanians who emigrated to the United States in the first quarter of the 20th century. The exact number of Albanian immigrants is unknown because most of them came to the United States before the independence of their home country, and consequently were listed by immigration authorities as Ottoman subjects. The best estimates in 1919 claimed that there were more than 40,000 Albanians in the United States, about 1,000 in Canada and the same number in Latin America. In Massachusetts alone, there were at least 10,000 Albanian immigrants.

All these Albanians came to America after 1900. Their numbers were swelled by an influx of refugees fleeing from Southern Albania after a Greek attack in 1914.

In analyzing the development of the Islamic Press in America, it should be kept in mind that a majority of early Muslim immigrants were illiterate, a fact which was characteristic of most immigrants from the old world journeying to the United States in search of opportunities. For example, when in 1906 the first Albanian newspaper *Kombi* came out, "not twenty persons out of the 5,000 Albanians could read or write." This newspaper was the organ of what later developed into the Albanian nationalist movement.

It is interesting to note that, at the time, close ties existed between orthodox Christian Albanians and Muslim Albanians living in the United States. During the formative years of the Albanian experience in America, Muslim Albanians were not particularly interested in setting up their own publications. Deeply involved in their nationalist struggle, most of them linked up with their Christian compatriots. Just as the orthodox Christian Albanians declared their religious independence from the Orthodox Greek Patriarch of Constantinople in 1908, so too the Muslim Albanians severed their ties with the Shaykh ul-Islam.

In addition to nationalist agitation, Albanians tried to increase the number of literates in their community by writing spelling books and newspapers which were made available to their countrymen for reading during the hours of rest following the hard daily work. As a result of such efforts, the number of literate Albanians increased to over 15,000.

A good illustration of the progress made in the United States by Albanians was the sharp increase in the number of Albanian newspapers and periodicals which appeared between 1906 and 1919. Except for the Albania, founded in 1918, almost all of the other thirteen publications were either nationalist organs or secularized outlets for the predominantly Christian Albanian community. Muslim Albanians at this time were organized by the Moslem National Alliance. This organization not only took charge of Muslim religious services, but it also undertook the education of illiterate Muslim Albanians. To this end, it established a school at Waterbury, Connecticut, and, according to contemporary reports, rendered invaluable services to the local Muslim community there.

Since the 1920s, Albanian Muslims have tried to maintain their Islamic heritage. With the influx of Muslims from other parts of the Islamic world, their sense of identity and solidarity with their brothers in Islam increased. In the 1950s, some Albanians in the midwestern part of the United States joined the Arab Lebanese and Syrian Muslims to form the International Muslim Society (later renamed the Federation of Islamic Associations). Their Muslim Star became the organ for the dissemination of Muslim news throughout the country. The Albanian majority also continued to build up their community through their own Albanian-language publications. In the post World War II period, Albanians ran the Islamic Educational Institute in New York. In July 1965, the Rabatah Journal reported the construction of a mosque and a center by Albanians. Assisted financially by their Arab-Muslim neighbors, the Albanians in Detroit also thrived.

Bosnian Muslims began migrating to the United States around the same time as the Albanians. Two factors contributed to the lack of effective newspaper and periodical reporting among the Bosnians. The first was the small number of Bosnians in America, and the second was their gradual assimilation into American society through intermarriages with Christians and especially other Slavic-speaking peoples (including Ukrainians, Slovaks and Croats).

Institution-building among the Bosnians, according to William G. Lockwood, became more evident in the fifties, when the arrival of new refugees led to a revival in Muslim-Bosnian consciousness. As a result of this development, the Bosnian-American Cultural Association (originally called the Muslim Religious and Cultural Home) was formed. In the late 1950s, this organization sponsored the only periodical (*Glasnik Muslimana*) published specifically for Bosnian Muslims in the United States, which lasted only a few years.

The last three decades have witnessed a significant growth in the number of American Muslim publications. Three types of Muslim publications can be identified in the United States. There are those published by Muslim national organizations, those identified with Islamic centers or local communities, and those printed by prison inmates who discovered Islam while serving jail terms. The first category of publication included the Darul Islam publications.

According to the September/October 1979 issue of *The Link*, the development of Islamic institutions and centers in the United States of America flourished during the 1950s. This was because of the small number of Muslims that had lived in America prior to that decade. The total population of Muslims in the United States was estimated at 30,000 in 1954 and somewhere around 100,000 in the early 1970s. The postwar efforts of Abdullah Ingram in Cedar Rapids, Iowa; Muhammad Omar in Quincy, Massachusetts; and J. Howar in Washington, D.C., resulted in the emergence of Muslim organizations throughout America.

The earliest recorded group to organize for communal prayer in private homes was in Ross, North Dakota in 1900. This group built a Mosque in 1920, but it did not publish any materials. Other centers emerged in Cedar Rapids, Highland Park, Michigan, Detroit (1922), and in New York (1922). This New York group, which was called the American Mohammedan Society, was founded in Brooklyn by Tartars. In 1923 an Arab organization called the Young Men's Muslim Association came into existence in the same area of New York City. To the best of our knowledge, no publication has been associated with these organizations.

In 1979/80 there were over 300 Islamic associations and mosques in the United States. Out of this figure, 100 belong to the American Muslim Missions. The members of these centers and mosques read the *American Muslim Journal* as their national publication. The most recent information available indicates that the Washington branch of the

American Muslim Mission is the only center which has tried to publish a local newspaper. Called the *al-Nur* (The Light), this paper has been appearing on an irregular basis. On a national level, besides the *American Muslim Journal* which appears weekly, there is also the *al-Qalam*, a monthly publication devoted to the analysis of social, cultural, economic and political issues in the United States. Articles in past issues of these journals demonstrate depth and understanding.

One of the most powerful groups of Muslims in the United States today is the Islamic Society of North America (an institutional outgrowth of the Muslim Student Association of North America). Serving as an umbrella for several Muslim organizations formerly linked to the Muslim Student Association (MSA), the Islamic Society of North America produces a number of publications through its various past constituents. The oldest and most prolific among these publications are the Muslim Student Association's *al-Ittihad* and *Islamic Horizons*, both of which were started almost two decades ago. The *al-Ittihad* is a quarterly journal, which features articles on various aspects of Islamic life in America and beyond. *Islamic Horizons* is more of a current affairs journal designed to keep the community abreast of developments around the world. For example, many articles in the 1980s focused on the Soviet invasion of Afghanistan and Muslim campaigns to improve the lot of their Afghan brethren. In addition to these Muslim Student Association publications, the Islamic Teaching Institute publishes journals and literature which provide guidance to Muslim organizations, Muslims in correctional institutions, and to Muslim and non-Muslim students in college campuses across the United States.

Apart from the publications of the Islamic Society of North America and the American Muslim Mission, some of the three hundred or more centers and mosques in America publish their own journals. The older Islamic centers pioneered Islamic journalism through their Newsletters and Bulletins. The Muslim Society in Cedar Rapids started the publication of the *Moslem World* over two decades ago, although this brainchild of Muhammad A. R. Webb's did not live through the 1960s. On the east coast, a center in Quincy, Massachusetts, started its own, *The Islamic Center of New England Newsletter* in 1957. This publication is still published regularly and its contents deal mainly with local Muslim community affairs and brief teachings from the Quran or the traditions of the Holy Prophet. In Washington, D. C., Dr. Abdul Rauf initiated *The*

Bulletin of the Islamic Center of Washington, which became a resource for the local community.

A long-lasting publication in the Detroit Muslim community has been the *American-Arab Message*, edited by Imam Muhammad Adib Karoub. A sibling if not a direct successor to *al-Hayat* (Life), the American-Arab Message follows the format of the older publication. Written both in Arabic and English, it devotes its limited pages to Arab affairs, to local community matters such as weddings and funerals, and to business and advertising.

In the western part of the United States sizable Muslim communities have developed in the last two decades. Several Muslim centers and mosques now exist in California. Two of these have established their own publications which are circulated widely. The first is *The Minaret* of the Islamic Center of Southern California. Published in Los Angeles, this bi-monthly journal is now in its third year. There is also a newsletter published by the Islamic Center of Sacramento, which is the oldest Muslim community on the West coast. This paper primarily serves the Pakistani/Indian Muslim Community in the western part of the United States. In the early period of Pakistani/Indian Muslim migration, the idea of an Islamic press was not considered because these immigrants were mainly agriculturalists who hoped that someday they would return home laden with the "golden fleece." Added to this fervent desire to strike it rich quickly and return to one's homeland was the pervasive discrimination encountered by Asians living and working in the western United States. Things improved for both Muslim South Asians and the prospect of a Western Islamic press after World War II, when barriers to citizenship and full enjoyment of the goods and services of the country were removed. These changes in United States policy and American attitudes led to the migration of greater numbers of South Asian Muslims. It is because of these significant developments that Muslim publications have flourished in the western United States.

The most recent addition to the growing list of publications published by the Islamic centers and mosques around the country, is the *Islamic Review*. Produced by the Ahmadiyya Anjuman Ishaat Islam of Lahore, Pakistan, this bi-monthly periodical is quite impressive. It will certainly successfully rival the *Muslim Sunrise* and the Ahmadiyya *Gazette*. The *Islamic Review* publishes articles dealing only with religious affairs. Unlike the equally impressive *Muslim Star* of the

Federation of Islamic Associations, it does not offer any political analysis of events in the *Muslim World*.

The most significant period in the growth of the Islamic press and
the proliferation of Islamic literature in the United States was the 1970s.
During this time a number of Muslim publications surfaced. The
Western Sunrise, edited by Imam Muhammad Tawfiq and dedicated to
explaining of Sunni Islam to native-born Americans, particularly Black
Americans, was published on the eastern seaboard. There was also the
al-Islam, an organ of the Islam Party of North America, which was
based in Washington, D.C. Both the *Western Sunrise* and the *al-Islam*
seem to be defunct today. During their brief existence both contributed
to the Islamization of a number of young Americans.

Another active but now defunct source of Islamic publications in
the United States was the Darul Islam Movement. This loose alliance of
Sunni mosques and Americans published the *al-Jihadul Akbar* and the
al-Nathir. Both gave news and analysis of the Muslim community. The
selection of writings by influential Muslims found in the two papers
revealed their affinity to al-Ghazzali, Sayed Qutb and other lesser religious scholars (*ulema*) of the Muslim world.

Three other publications in the eastern seaboard are *The Islamic
Revolution, The New Muslim Outlook,* and *The Islam*. The first is a child
of the Iranian revolution, for its origins date back to the eruption of that
event when it represented the efforts of Iranian militants to articulate
their views in America. The second is a recent development in the
Islamic community and its message is radical and fundamentalist. The
third is a publication of the Muslim Development Corporation in
Alexandria, Virginia. It provides an outlet for that organization's plans
to develop the Muslim community in the area.

One of the quarterlies that has become a very important scholarly
outlet for Muslims and their intellectual products is *The Search*, a journal of Arab/Islamic Studies. This publication is based in Vermont and
edited by Dr. Samir Robbo, and has in its brief life span of three years
published articles on Islam in America, Islam in Africa, Palestinian
rights, Jerusalem and Israeli occupation, and other areas of interest
specifically to the Arab and Muslim reader.

In the mid-western part of the United States, some new publications
have surfaced in the past decade or two. The newsletter of the Islamic
Cultural Center of Greater Chicago publishes a newsletter. Edited by

Imam K.Y. Avdick, this publication has become an important source of information, as well as a link between the various members of the Yugoslavian community in America. Its format consists of editorial and other sections devoted to religious and ethical issues in American society. Another journal based in Chicago is *The Message*, a publication of the Muslim Community Center there.

There are also several publications that appeared in the last decade in California. One of the significant developments in the history of the Muslim press in America is the creation of the *Muslim Business Development Forum* (Palo Alto, California). A publication of the Association of Muslim Businessmen and Professionals, this periodical covers business affairs in the Muslim world. It identifies Muslim businessmen through a "Who's Who" column and facilitates communication and dialogue in a section called "Open Forum." Further it carries a calendar of events and a page for classified advertisements.

Another new publication that has appeared and circulated in California is the monthly *al-Bayan Bulletin*. An organ of the Association of Concerned Muslims at Berkeley, this paper covers international news from a radical Muslim perspective. It is a companion to the quarterly by the same name.

Before concluding this survey of the history of the Islamic press in the United States of America, reference should be made to two categories of papers which deserve attention. The first category includes publications put out by Shiite groups in the United States. A list of such papers includes *Islamic Affairs* (a publication of the Islamic Society of Georgia), *Islamic Review* (a monthly that was started in the 1970s by the members of the Shia Association of North America (SANA)), and a bimonthly magazine called *The Message of Islam*, edited by Shaikh Muhammad Sarwar. This last publication has been described by another Shiite paper as irregular. Nevertheless, its irregularity does not negate the fact that it carries an excellent introduction to the Islamic classical literature that is still to be translated for public reading. The *Husaini News* is another irregular newsletter that serves as a forum for the Shiite in the midwest and beyond.

The Ansarullah Movement in the United States is one of the most prolific producers of "Islamic literature." Since the early seventies it has published a monthly paper which covers a wide range of issues. In each issue, there are articles dealing with Quranic interpretations and translations, and quotes from the Christian scriptures which Imam Isa al-Mahdi argued must be read alongside the Quran to fathom the depths of the divine message. This Ansarullah paper also prints columns dealing extensively with current social, economic and cultural problems in American life and society. One recent example is an article on American music and the seductive nature of some popular songs.

The other category is composed of papers published by inmates who have embraced Islam while serving their sentences in American jails. In recent years many of these converts, mostly Black Americans, have requested more information on Islam and have joined hands with fellow inmates to set up newspapers. Such publications are usually used as windows to the outside world or as a meeting point among the inmates themselves.

The Islamic press in America has traveled a long way. Muslims who want to be informed about events from a Muslim perspective can now sample from a growing number of locally published Muslim publications. The nature of technological civilization in America will most likely continue to encourage Muslim use of the media to advance the cause of Islam. In this manner, the Islamic press in America will expand and grow. Such a result will benefit Muslims and non-Muslims alike.

8
ISLAM AND THE CONTEMPORARY CHALLENGES IN NORTH AMERICA

There are now at least 6 million Muslims living in North America. That is to say that here are 5 million Muslims in the U. S. and at least one million of their counterparts and co-religionists in Canada. This size and diversity of the Muslim community in North America causes one to wonder what constituent groups comprise this community and how it came into being. In order to answer these questions and to deal with the question of challenges facing this section of the global Muslim Community (*ummah*), one needs more time than has been allotted to me. But in this time, I will try to give you a brief historical sketch of the community as well as identify a few of the challenges facing the Muslims in North America.

According to two recent studies done separately by the American Muslim Council (AMC) in Washington D.C. and the Islamic Resource Institute of California, Muslims in Canada alone have at least 250 mosques and centers, whereas in the U.S. they have at least four times that figure with over 1,000 mosques and centers. Together that makes more than 1,250 mosques and centers in all of North America, a remarkable achievement for a community whose members were counted in the thousands as recently as the 1950s. Three factors have contributed to this growth; immigration, natural birth and conversion. And as a result, we now have Muslims from all predominantly Muslim countries and from all parts of the world where Muslims are in the minorities, as well as native-born Americans and Canadians who have converted to the natural religion (*din al-fitra*). Some came by way of the Nation of Islam; some were independent seekers of the truth and of divine guidance who discovered Islam in their spiritual journeys; others simply married Muslims and later embraced Islam. Nonetheless, all of these members contribute to the unique diversity of the Muslim community.

It is indeed against this background of growth and diversity that we examine the challenges facing the Muslim community in North America. The first challenge which arises is the question of identity. This is an important question because a person's identity puts him or her in a triangular relationship with himself, with his community and with the significant others who lump him or her with those he or she identifies with or is perceived to identify with. In North America, the Muslim community faces an identity challenge in three separate areas of life. There is first the element of conflict from the political arena where anti-Muslim factions are constantly trying to paint Muslims in negative terms, trying to effectively maintain the perception of the Muslims as the marginalized other, those who should not be accepted as a part of North American society because of the threat they constitute. This identity challenge parallels that which was posed by the Meccans to the small Islamic community in Mecca. At the time of the Prophet the propagandists of the Meccans and their cohorts among the Arabian tribes claimed that the Muslims were troublemakers who challenged their beliefs and threatened their way of life. This argument was not only made by the Meccans in Arabia but also in Abyssinia where the Muslim emigrants had sought refuge during the first hijrah. It should be recalled that when 'Amar Ibn al-As Ibn Wail and Abdullah Ibn Abu Kabia were sent to Abyssinia to convince the Negus al-Bahar (The Sea-King) to return the Muslim refugees, they, according to a hadith reported by Um Salama, made their charge against the Muslim refugees in the following manner:

> Some foolish fellows from our people have taken
> refugee in the king's country. They have forsaken our religion
> and not accepted yours, but have brought in an invented reli-
> gion which neither we nor you know anything about. Our
> nobles have sent us to the King to get him to return them.

In order to get the generals of the king to go with their scheme, the Meccan delegates took with them presents of the choicest wares of Mecca, especially the leather work which Abyssinians valued greatly.

There is much for North American Muslims to learn from this

episode in the Sirah as well as from the reply of Jafar Ibn Abi Talib to the Negus question regarding their faith. The spokesperson of the Muslim's delegation not only affirmed their belief in the unity of God and the spiritual, social and moral transformation of the Islamic revolution brought in by the Prophet, but he also demonstrated the constant need for Muslims anywhere to combine the principles of missionary work and dialogue within the framework of Islamic belief and practice. To defend the Muslims from the slander and calumny of the Meccans, according to the sirah literature, Jafar made the following speech:

> O King, we were an uncivilized people, worshipping idols, eating corpses, committing abominations, breaking natural ties, treating guests badly, and our strong devoured the weak. Thus we were until God sent us an apostle whose lineage, truth, trustworthiness, and clemency we know. He summoned us to acknowledge God's unity and to worship him and renounce the stones, and images which we and our fathers formerly worshiped. He commanded us to speak the truth, be faithful to our engagements, mindful of the ties of kinship and kindly hospitality, and to refrain from crimes and bloodshed. He forbade us to commit abominations and to speak lies, and to devour the property of orphans, to vilify chaste women. He commanded us to worship God alone and not to associate anything with Him, and he gave us orders about prayer, alms-giving, and fasting (enumerating the Commands of Islam). We confessed his truth and believe in him, and we followed him in what he had brought from God, and we worshiped God alone without association (aught) with Him. We treated as forbidden what he forbade, and as lawful what he declared lawful. Thereupon our people attacked us, treated us harshly and seduced us from our fait hto try to make us go back to the worship of idols instead of the worship of God, and to regard as lawful the evil deeds we once committed so when they got the better of us, treated us unjustly and circumscribed our lives, and came between us and our religion, we came to your country, having chosen you above all others. Here we have him happy in your protection, and we hope that we shall not be treated unjustly while we are with you, O King.

Jafar's words bear significant relevance to modern-day North

American Muslims. Like Jafar and his contemporaries, they must also battle with political enemies who are continually trying to influence authorities to take negative actions against them and, like Jafar and his companions in Abyssinia, the Muslims must recognize that associating partnership with Allah (*shirk*) has not disappeared completely in human society. In the western world today, in place of idols made out of stones and gravel images, modern nonbelievers have substituted conceptual images. The most visible location of the new idols is in the realm of popular culture. The preoccupation with material things has now philosophically changed the attitude of many human beings towards this world and the next. Convinced that materiality is the only reality for human beings, modern man has put the Cartesian dictum (I think, therefore I am) on its head. Unlike Descartes who said, "I think, therefore I am," popular thinkers now identify with the "Yuppies," "Buppies" and the "Muppies" of North America (or Yummies as they are called in the U. K.) and put forth a different philosophy of life. To them, owning is the essence of life. Hence, their dictum: "I own, therefore, I am." This view of life defines their identity strictly in material terms. Even though such people ascend in social systems and maintain contacts with different people, their life is defined strictly in material terms and seeming to define a part of their identity while these other components of their life are seen as extensions of their own egos.

This philosophical attitude of the "Yuppies" or "Muppies" and their like pose a challenge with regards to the cultural life of the North American Muslim and in order for them to face up to this challenge, cultural strategies of survival must be developed. In order for Muslim men and women to maintain their identities, their mental furniture must remain untampered and unsoiled by the negative forces around them.

A third and final area of life in which the Muslim identity is threatened is in the economic sphere. In the domain of the marketplace, buying and selling is the order of the day. Muslims must register their presence in this domain if the Muslim community in North America is to make any significant breakthrough in the economic sphere, it must take note of the implications of the underlying philosophy of the new capitalists whose reality is defined by the market forces, cyberspace and the compulsive power to possess and own things material.

9

RECENT TRENDS IN AMERICAN MEDIA COVERAGE OF ISLAM AND MUSLIMS IN THE UNITED STATES OF AMERICA

INTRODUCTION

Prior to the Iranian Revolution, American newspapers and the public media generally reported negatively about the Muslim World. The press in the United States was subject to occasional outbursts of anger and emotionalism resulting from isolated events in the Muslim world. Scholars familiar with the Middle East and the Muslim world attributed these anti-Muslim sentiments to the spill-over effects of the Arab/Israeli war or to the traditional Christian hostility towards Muslims which grew out of the Crusades.

Even while such hostile sentiments were prevalent, they were being countered by U. S. propaganda efforts to woo Muslims away from the communist influence in the Middle East. U. S. publications and the Voice of America broadcasts tried to put the East/West conflict in religious terms, and Muslims were portrayed in many instances as ideological cousins of the West. Some Western scholars lent their intellectual support to this claim, and soon articles and books began to introduce terms like Judeo-Christian-Islamic cultures. Others simply lumped together Jews, Christians and Muslims as members of a single community following the Abrahamic tradition.

Also interesting at this time was the impact of secularism on the Western perception of Islam and Muslim society. During the post-World War II period, many American scholars and journalists writing about Islam and the Muslim world accepted the dominant contemporary view that modernization was in vogue worldwide. They saw Third

119

World leaders as bent on transforming their societies into mirror images of the West. Secure in their belief that modernization was the dream of all developing countries, and working on the assumption that religion was losing its luster and strength in the Third World, reporters and scholars began to talk about "the passing of traditional society."

Nevertheless, hostility between religions persisted. Indeed, it was the violent and irrational outburst of hostility towards Muslims that led Edward Said of Columbia University to write his now celebrated book, *Covering Islam*. For those who are seriously interested in fostering dialogue between the religious communities of the world there is a sense of urgency in dealing with the fallout of slanted and hostile media coverage and its negative implications for Christian-Muslim relations and the diplomatic efforts of the United States.

This essay will discuss media treatment of issues relating to Islam and the Muslim world since the Iranian Revolution. The sources consulted consist of newspapers, Christian and Jewish magazines and scholarly journals included in the Index of Religious Literature. Working on the assumption that these publications are widely read, and that the messages contained therein affect the thinking and attitudes of readers, this report examines them with the sole purpose of extrapolating possible implications for Christian-Muslim relations and Jewish-Muslim relations.

CHRISTIAN PUBLICATIONS AND THEIR COVERAGE OF ISLAM AND THE MUSLIM WORLD

In looking at media coverage by Christian communities in America, one must bear in mind the fact that there is a wide variety of Christian publications. Missionary publications are designed to promote the Christian faith and to report glowingly on the spread of Christianity in the world beyond the United States of America. Other Christian publications are written to address local issues, while still others deal with doctrinal matters and hardly address Christian-Muslim issues.

Christian media coverage does not take place in a vacuum. There is a context and a background that affect the nature and content of reporting. Missionary magazines in 1979 used developments in Iran as a justification to request additional contributions from Christian congregations to fund a more aggressive campaign against the "fanatics of Islam." Events in Iran caused local-issue publications to become more attentive to the global stirrings of Islam. While doctrinal publications did not change in their format and coverage, a few attempted a comparative analysis of Islam and Christianity. With articles often written by Muslims living in the West or by Christian scholars writing from the Third World, *The Muslim World* from the Hartford Theological Seminary has provided some of the best writings in this area of comparison.

In America, these developments and coverage took place during the rise of the New Right and Christian fundamentalism of the Rev. Jerry Falwell variety. These two movements created an atmosphere suited to negative Christian media coverage of *The Muslim World*. Members of the New Right, whose credentials as legitimate conservatives have been challenged by many old-time American conservatives, argued for a tougher American attitude towards Third World radical regimes. They advocated greater use of American military power in dealing with groups and countries opposed to the United States.

What even now frightens many American advocates of the separation of church and state is the verbal blurring of the line between the two in the rhetoric of the New Right and their Christian fundamentalist fellow travelers. Three points need to be addressed regarding this issue: the attitude of the New Right and other fundamentalists towards Israel, their idea of Islam and *The Muslim World*, and their views on the employment of military power in world politics.

With regard to the opinion of the New Right regarding the state of Israel, there is undisputed evidence of overwhelming support. Nevertheless, it should be noted that support for the Jewish state is conditioned by biblical considerations, which take precedence over political interests. There are differences between the secular New Right members and the Bible-inspired fundamentalists in their reasoning behind this stance on Israel. The secular New Right entertains the notion that Israel is a democracy and shares a community of historical tradition with the West. For this and other related reasons, the United States has a vested interest in supporting this state against its Arab enemies. Many of these New Right members are politicians, and their support is invariably determined by the political realization that the Jewish lobby can make or break them. Christian fundamentalists, on the other hand, are motivated by a different agenda. Their support for the Jewish state is based on millenarian and dispensationist expectations. Working on the assumption that the end of time is near, and that their Saviour Jesus Christ is about to return to earth, many fundamentalists see in the Creation of Israel the fulfillment of prophecy. A whole genre of literature in the Christian community deals with this issue. Authors like Hal Lindsey and preachers such as the late Herbert W. Armstrong of *Plain Truth* fame are both examples of writers who have followed this way of thinking. Lindsey, whose books have sold by the millions, is one of the main figures responsible for the widespread belief that the coming of the state of Israel is the beginning of the fulfillment of prophecy. Though his predictions have not come true, his message is still publicized among millenarians and dispensationists awaiting the return of Christ. Although Armstrong's brand of rigid fundamentalism had been producing literature of this type long before the emergence of the New Right in America, such millenarian ideas dominated the media and the airwaves in the mid-1970s.

These developments were significant because of the implications they had for American politics and for the development of attitudes in America towards *The Muslim World*, where Israel was supposedly struggling against the Muslims and Islam. With the wide circulation of such ideas in the late 1960s and early 1970s we witnessed the coming to power of a new breed of American politicians who stressed their Christian background and their commitment to that heritage. The election of Jimmy Carter to the White House brought the first born-again Christian to the presidency. This train of events changed the political and religious climate in the country. In an editorial in the *Journal of Christian Studies*, James E. Wood discussed the similarities and differences between religious fundamentalists and the New Right. What is evident from this analysis is that, although there are differences between the two groups where issues relating to domestic matters are concerned, there is clearly a unanimity of views on the Middle East. Nevertheless, the rationale for support of the Jewish state varies from person to person and group to group within the larger New Right/Fundamentalist Coalition.

While President Carter introduced the born-again Christian viewpoint to the national stage in the early and mid 1970s, President Ronald Reagan was instrumental in creating the atmosphere of suspicion and hostility among American conservatives (New Right and fundamentalists) with regard to *The Muslim World*. His open courting of fundamentalists and the New Right and his free use of phrases from the Bible lent support to the view that the President saw America as a Christian nation in which Christian values must be cultivated. Reagan's views on the importance of scripture were made clear in the March 3, 1983 issue of *CT*, a conservative Christian publication.

A curious development that can be seen in publications of Christian communities at the time, was the new partnership between fundamentalists and Jews. This alliance attracted the attention of writers, and led to the publication of articles such as David Rausch's "Fundamentalism and the Jews," in the *Journal of Evangelical Theology* (1980). By the late 1970's, fundamentalist Christian publications had solidly rallied behind Israel. Their positive coverage of the Jewish state was echoed by the electronic media.

But if Muslims were concerned about this train of events, so were mainstream Christian churches, although for different reasons. Writing in the Baptist publication *Foundation* (April/June, 1982), William G. McLoughlin revealed the illusions and dangers of the New Christian Right to the wider American community. Although the author recognized the legitimacy and relevance of the issues raised by fundamentalists and New Right Christians, he cautioned his fellow Americans to be aware of hidden dangers. He also reminded fundamentalists that their claim to leadership of the evangelical movement was shaky, and that their ability to deliver to the 31 million evangelicals was doubtful.

Even if this assessment of the Christian Right is correct, its uncritical acceptance of the pro-Israeli position of these groups makes it difficult for a Christian-Muslim dialogue to take place. The New Right's millenarian view of the state of Israel makes it blind and deaf to the realities of the Palestinian situation. In their jubilant expectation of the contemporary fulfillment of their biblical prophecies, these Christians are willing to forget the plight of the Palestinians. This makes a Christian-Muslim dialogue even less likely.

The only way out of this impasse is to demystify the claims of those who believe in the imminent end of time. The peddlers of this Armageddon syndrome are politically dangerous because they not only promote millenarian and dispensationist ideas, but also encourage a dangerous kind of militarism. The very threat they pose to the larger community of mankind makes their claims spurious and insupportable. Cooler heads among Christians and Muslims, working together, can positively affect the train of events in the country. Hopefully, in the long run, even Jewish leaders would join such a call for rationality and dialogue among believers in the Abrahamic tradition, in order to avoid a global war.

A step in the right direction is the de-mystification of the ideas of men like Lindsey in Samuel Bacchiocchi's recent article on "Are We in the Countdown to Armageddon?," published in the March 1986 issue of *Signs of the Times*. Bacchiocchi puts it well when he writes: "Lindsey's excessive preoccupation with spying out the future by constructing a prophetic jigsaw puzzle of the last-day events can adversely affect both Christian faith and practice. It can lead us to fasten our attention on impersonal events rather than to look for personal Saviour. To base our conviction that Jesus is coming soon on the changeable world of events rather than on the unchangeable reality of God's love means that we wait, not for a personal Saviour, but for impersonal events—the establishment of the state of Israel. . . ." Views such as these are crucial in the preparation for a meaningful dialogue between Christians and Muslims. The de-mystification of millenarian and dispensationist ideas would not only sharpen the realities of the Middle East situation, but would also be accepted by those Orthodox Jews who do not see the hand of God in the creation of Israel after the Second World War.

It is only in this context that dialogue can take place. If The Synagogue Council of America (SCA), which represents Conservative, Orthodox and Reform Judaism, is serious about meeting members of other faiths to discuss "terrorism," it must also deal with its approach to the notion that the creation of the Jewish state was the fulfillment of divine prophecy.

Besides the dangers associated with exaggerating biblical prophecy, there is also the danger of raising false alarms against Muslims living in the West. Since the Iranian Revolution, much derisive and distorted news about Muslims and Islam has appeared in the Christian press of the United States of America. The tables of contents of many of these publications at the time of the Iranian revolution show several articles in each issue which reflect this attitude. One article in Christianity Today in March, 1980, was entitled, "Why are Muslims so Militant: They Have Set Out to Bring The Rest Of The World To Submit To Allah and His Prophet." Written by Don M. Curry, this piece set out to turn its readers against Muslims and Islam. Articles such as this one were seen throughout the country, and damaged any residue of goodwill between the U. S. and her Muslim friends in the non-Communist world.

Cooler heads among the main line churches took a more cautious approach to the fallout from the Iranian Revolution. Even the editors of *Christianity Today* recognized the responsibility of Christians in the wake of such violent uprising in the Middle East. In an April, 1979 piece, entitled "Islamic Fundamentalism and Christian Responsibility," Byron Haines touched on some of the key issues that are likely to affect the nature of Muslim-Christian relations.

One great danger to Christian-Muslim relations is the publication of articles in Christian magazines which are likely to jeopardize the lives of Muslims in the West. A good illustration of this new trend can be found in a recent article by an American author of Egyptian Coptic descent. In an essay entitled "Islam: Danger at Our Doorstep," Michael Youssef writes in an alarmist manner, summoning American Christians to get up and fight the Muslims in their midst. With intent to alarm he writes:

> Most of us are aware that Islamic fundamentalism
> has something to do with terrorism in the Middle East. But
> are we aware of the threat that exists here in our own coun-
> try to us as Christians?

Such statements belie the fact that America is a pluralistic society. Muslim Americans do not pose a threat to their fellow citizens and, as a minority, it makes little sense for them to employ violence. Islam has progressed in this country through peaceful means and no major Muslim publication or author of note has advocated anything different. It is unconstitutional and politically imprudent to lash out against American Muslims to express grievances against Muslim fundamentalists elsewhere in the world.

JEWISH MEDIA AND THE COVERAGE OF ISLAM AND THE MUSLIM WORLD: THE IMPLICATIONS FOR AMERICAN-MUSLIM RELATIONS

Prior to the creation of Israel, American Jews did not have strong negative attitudes towards Arabs and Islam. Yet, today, there is marked hostility between the two groups, due to the creation of Israel and the generation of warfare that has now characterized Arab/Jewish relations worldwide.

It is against this background that Jewish publications are examined to shed light on media coverage of Muslims and Islam in America. Although some Christian churches welcomed the coming into existence of Israel, Christian enthusiasm was limited during the formative period of the Jewish state. Things changed after the war in June 1967 and growing reports of Muslim-Christian tension in places like Lebanon. In fact, the 1967 War and the Israeli occupation of Jerusalem marked a major turning point in Jewish self-confidence and in Jewish prowess in the wider world. A careful examination of Jewish press reports shows that after the 1967 War, the Jewish media increasingly stressed Israel as a part of the West. Tours were organized by American travel agencies for Americans eager to see the Promised Land they had heard so much about from their Sunday School teachers. With these developments, Israel began to gain an audience among evangelicals and fundamentalists. As mentioned in the previous section, many evangelicals and fundamentalists who saw the recapture of Jerusalem from Muslim hands as a sign of the fulfillment of Biblical prophecy began to write about Israel in favorable terms. The writings of Jewish reporters and intellectuals echoed and reinforced what was also appearing in the secular and Christian press.

Between 1967 and 1976, when President Carter came to the White House, the American Jewish media had succeeded in creating an alliance with fundamentalists in the U. S. This new alignment was made possible by a certain train of events in the country. The first was the phenomenon of the "Jews for Jesus" movement. After two thousand years of bitterness in Christian-Jewish relations, young Jews now clamored for admission into the fold of Christ, who had been rejected by their ancestors. This was a step towards Christian reconciliation with a Jewish community that was now tolerant enough to accept the "defection" of some of its young people. Another development which encouraged the Judeo-Christian alliance was the rise of the Moral Majority. In an interesting article Bruce H. Joffe wrote about "Jews Who Believe in Jesus." Here the author addresses the dilemma such converts to Christianity faced while making good their commitment to the Nazarene from Bethlehem. Because conversion was such a challenge, Joffe felt that Jews for Jesus needed to develop a balance to live with their faith while still maintaining their Jewish identity. In another piece, M. H. Tannenbaum raised the issue of whether or not the Moral Majority is good for Jews. His piece in the *Hadassah Magazine* of April, 1981 expressed the feelings of Jews who were cautious about the fundamentalist embrace.

Fearful or not, by the mid-1970s American Jews were now being embraced by Christian fundamentalists. This new state of mind among Christian fundamentalists led Webb Blitzer to ask an important question in his article entitled, "The Christian Right-Friend or Foe?" This piece, which was printed in the *National Jewish Monthly* of April 1981 serves as a companion to the Tannenbaum article.

While the religious publications of the Jewish community were engaged in reflections on the New Right and the Moral Majority, some more secular Jewish groups were doing battle with the Muslims and Islam. Writing in the June 1984 issue of *Commentary*, Bernard Lewis examined the question of Jews living in Muslim lands. After examining the history of Jews in Islamic areas of the Middle East, he concluded that the present trend is towards what he called "Muslim Anti-semitism." One must keep in mind that *Commentary*, which has over the last ten years carved out a niche for itself as an organ of the Neo-conservatives and the New Right, generally portrays Islam and Muslims in a negative light. The opinions expressed in this magazine were later reproduced in other Jewish weeklies and monthlies throughout the U.S. Some of these views spread in the wider American media, interestingly enough almost always through secular organs such as the *New York Times* or *The Washington Post*.

THE AMERICAN SECULAR PRESS AND ITS COVERAGE OF MUSLIMS AND ISLAM

There are four themes that are most widely dealt with in the American media when it covers Muslims and Islam. The first is the Arab-Israeli conflict, the second is Islamic fundamentalism, the third is the question of terrorism in *The Muslim World* and the last is the lack of development in the Muslim world.

A systematic review of the Bell and Howell Index to the most important American dailies (*The New York Times, The Washington Post, The Los Angeles Times, The Chicago Tribune* and *The Christian Science Monitor*) shows that each of these papers reported on the Arab/Israeli conflict more than fifty times every month. Their perceptions of the problem seem to be uniform, although *The Christian Science Monitor* diverges from general coverage on certain issues. Although almost all papers recognize that the Arab-Israeli conflict is not necessarily based on religion, the struggle in the region has been treated as purely religio-political since the Iranian Revolution. The Arab-Israeli conflict has taken many forms since the original confrontation at the time of the creation of the Jewish state. After the 1967 War, the American media began paying greater attention to the region and coverage became more and more politicized. The Jewish lobby in the country has become very sensitive to newspaper accounts of the conflict, and articles that are not pro-Israeli are challenged. Such challenges take the form of counter-articles or letters to the editor.

In covering the Arab-Israeli conflict over the last twenty years, U. S. newspapers have gradually split the issue into two, namely, the war between the front line Arab states (Jordan, Egypt—until Camp David—and Syria) and the Palestinian Problem. The media has come to focus more on the activities of the Palestinians than on the original issues of the Arab-Israeli conflict. While giving the Palestinian issue primary coverage, the U. S. media has characterized Palestinians as terrorists who hijack planes, bomb buildings and take hostages. From 1969 to 1973, the image of the Palestine Liberation Organization was that of the bloody perpetrator of violence against Israelis, Jews and other support-ers of Israel around the world. The association of the PLO with Islam and Muslims became stronger following the Iranian Revolution, when Imam Khomeini gave the Israeli Embassy in Tehran to the PLO. Many western reporters began to associate the PLO and Islam in general. To them Arab terrorism and Islamic terrorism in Iran became bedfellows.

U. S. reporters popularized the Iranian Revolution during the hostage crisis. Scholars, too, gave the Revolution greater attention in comments to the media and scholarly presentations after the crisis began. Thus, regardless of one's attitudes towards Islamic fundamental-ism, it has become one of the much talked about and much discussed phenomena in American political life. As a result of the extensive media coverage, the American public is becoming more and more conditioned to believe that Islamic fundamentalism is part of the Palestinian Problem, which is in turn a part of the Arab-Israeli conflict. This per-ception of the middle eastern reality is a distortion which the media has fostered. Unless those who are seriously interested in a Christian-Muslim dialogue help change the American attitude toward Islam, the chances for a peaceful resolution of the conflict are very slim. Without this adjustment, prospects for U. S. diplomatic success in the Arab and Muslim world will gradually dim in the years to come.

What is disturbing about recent news coverage of Islam and the Muslim world in the American media is the emerging view that Islam = Arabs = fundamentalism = terrorism. This is a good indication of the confusion among those who interpret events abroad for the American public. By confusing Islam with Arab nationalism, with a certain segment of the Muslim community, or with terrorism, news commentators and reporters have done a great disservice to Muslims and their religion. One of the earliest articles appearing in the American media which helped create hostility and suspicion between Americans and the Muslims (particularly Iranians) was Steven Stasser's "Khomeini Contagion," which appeared in the December 17, 1979 issue of *Newsweek*. Since the publication of these first writings in the aftermath of the Iranian Revolution Americans have come to accept the barrage of pieces denigrating Islam. The deliberate association of Islam with terrorism in the Middle East has made it more and more difficult to separate the two in serious discussions with Americans who have been conditioned by the media. This recent development in the American press, which can be better understood after a careful analysis of the articles on Islam and terrorism contained in the Bell and Howell Index, has poisoned the climate of opinion in the country. Those who are working toward Muslim-Christian dialogue have faced an uphill struggle to stem the tide of suspicion and redirect American attention to the real issue, the Palestinian question in the Middle East.

Three explanations could account for the approach of the American media to Islam and the Middle East. First, there is the misconception that all Arabs are Muslims. Secondly, the Lebanese Crisis, which originally pitted Muslims and Christians, has continued to reflect animosity between the two religious communities. Lastly, there is a notion that any group in the Middle East that employs violence must be Muslim. This last factor has resulted in cases where violence perpetrated by non-Muslims has been identified as acts of Islamic fundamentalism.

The mistaken idea that all Arabs are Muslims and that Arab nationalism is synonymous with all things Islamic has been encouraged by the

American media. Until the 1973 War and the eruption of the Lebanese Civil War, American reporters did not portray the Middle East conflict as a religious war. Some reports suggested religious undercurrents, but no effort was made to characterize the conflict as a religious war between Jews and Muslims. At that time, it was not in the interests of the Israeli leadership to project such an image, for it would have cost Israel much support in the Muslim world, where it had many diplomatic ties. It was the religious nature of the 1973 War between the Arabs and the Israelis which led to a greater emphasis on the religious content of the conflict. In keeping with this new religious focus, the 1973 conflict came to be called "The Ramadan War" by the Muslims and the "Yom Kippur War" by the Jews. Scholars and journalists who try to steer clear of these religiously inspired names use the term "October War of 1973."

The Lebanese crisis has given rise to three important perceptions which have had serious consequences for Muslims. First, it has created a climate of suspicion between the two religious communities. Christian missionary groups now assume that there are potential "Lebanons" elsewhere in the world. This climate of suspicion and animosity must be checked if the Christian and Muslim communities wish to engage in meaningful dialogue.

A second perception that has developed is that all terrorist acts in the Middle East are perpetrated by Muslims. Recent articles on terrorism in *The New York Times* and *The Washington Post* have contributed to this erroneous perception. Groups such as the so-called Islamic Jihad and Hizbullah (basically Shiite groups) are talked about as if they represent the entire Community (*ummah*) (Muslim Commonwealth) in both thought and deed.

But if the Lebanese crisis and the numerous associated contradictions created conditions for a growing confusion about Islam and Muslims in the American mind, the emergence of Muammar Qaddafi of Libya as an international leader has also only worsened the situation. The American media treated the Libyan Revolution largely as a nationalist phenomenon. After the Iran-Iraq War broke out, many Arab states, including Libya and Syria, rallied behind Iran. Confused and unable to interpret this new reality, American reporters latched on to the only thing that seemingly united Syrians, Libyans and Iranians: their common belief in Islam. This seems to be a weak reason for associating all of

Islam with terrorism. The negative perception of Muslims and Islam is responsible for the poor state of relations between the U. S. government and the three governments identified above. The 1986 U. S. bombing of strategic targets in the North African state dramatized in the most dangerous way the high level of tension between the U. S. and Libya under Qaddafi. Such an atmosphere of suspicion and hostility could soon create tension and possibly war between the U. S. and Syria as well.

Regardless of how one views events in the Middle East, perceptions will continue to be affected by media reporting. Unless the psychological associations existing in the minds of Americans are overcome, no meaningful or fruitful dialogue can be initiated. It is imperative for Christian leadership in America to come together with Muslim leaders in America and abroad to establish a dialogue on these important issues. To work for such a goal is not only good from a religious standpoint, but is also politically sound.

10
THE THEOLOGY OF THE "OTHER" IN ISLAM: AN AMERICAN MUSLIM PERSPECTIVE

The contemporary world in which we live is now generally accepted as a "televillage." This term implies that mankind lives very close to one another. Although people around the globe are separated by oceans and seas, the distances between them have been bridged by technological breakthroughs we have made over the last one hundred years. These technological and scientific developments have indeed created a new social universe whose residents must now learn to live together and to spend greater time trying to understand one another. The religious traditions of humankind have for centuries provided an intellectual, psychological and social framework within which men, women and children have learned over the years to deal with each other as brothers and sisters. Religious settings and environments have also created tragic situations which pitted one group against another. Because of this mixed bag of interreligious communication and miscommunication, an effort has been made in this century to bridge what was considered a gulf separating members of one faith community from the other. The negative tendency in human communication regarding religious traditions is being challenged and corrected by those of us who are committed to dialogue and to the dialogue process. As I have argued elsewhere, this dialogue process, to which I am fully committed, has been made possible largely by the secularization of human society and by the increasing material and social transformation of human living. Humanity today is condemned to live in a world of ever changing technology, and forced to reconcile itself to the demands of a

133

material culture which is increasingly responsible for the desacrilization of human life and its physical environment. In light of these conditions, humankind has come to see secularization as a necessary "evil" whose destructive powers can be harnessed for the maintenance of political legitimacy of rulers and for the development of a public square where each faith community is allowed to exist undisturbed, as long as it does not interfere with the right of others to exist as well.

ON THE DIFFERENCE BETWEEN MUSLIMS AND NON-MUSLIMS

In the religion of Islam, there are numerous verses in the Holy Quran which make it categorically clear that Muslims are different from other humans. A Muslim is generally known as the human being who has decided without any doubt in his or her mind that there is only one God (Allah) and that Muhammad is His Messenger. This definition of the Muslim is based on two principles. The first is the principle of *tawhid* (unity or oneness of God); the second is the principle of prophethood (*nubuwwah*). The Holy Quran states that true believers are those who accept the doctrine of radical monotheism, the messengership of the Holy Prophet Muhammad, and the holy books of the ancient prophets such as Abraham, Moses and Jesus. According to the Holy Quran, Muslims are those who believe in the hereafter, the day of the resurrection, the day of judgement, hell and heaven, the angels of God and the existence of Satan, the accursed. Because of these criteria, Islam recognizes a distinction between humans like Christians and Jews who believe in one God and humans who are completely cut off from the world of believers in *tawhid*. Members of the Christian and Jewish communities who believe in one God are generally referred to as *ahl al-kitab* (People of the Book). These Christian and Jewish peoples are generally treated differently from unbelievers who totally and uncompromisingly reject the teachings of the prophets. According to Muslim traditions, which are based on the Holy Quran itself, God dispatched a prophet to each and every people of the world. The difference between Islam and the other monotheistic religions, according to Muslim belief, lies in the fact that, in their original forms, the Jewish and Christian communities received revelations from the prophets sent to them by God. However, over several generations, the original messages revealed to the members of these two communities were distorted. Hence the coming of the last and final revelation through the Holy Prophet

Muhammad. This idea of the corruption of earlier revelations to humanity has led Muslims to another belief, based on the Holy Quran, which states that the final revelation is protected from corruptibility by God himself. This Muslim distinction between the *ahl al-kitab* and themselves has given rise to three different categories of human attitudes toward the Transcendent.

First, there are those who embrace *tawhid* and are guided in their daily lives by the moral compass of Islam. Socialized into Islam and determined to obtain the blessings of the Almighty, these believers are described by the Holy Quran as the companions of the right in the hereafter. In this life, they believe in the unseen (*ghaib*), offer their daily prescribed prayers, enjoin what is good and forbid what is evil. Such believers do good deeds and fear their Creator and the Day of Reckoning.

There is a second category of humans who believe in the Creator, but because they belong to a faith community whose original message has been corrupted, their communication with the Creator is confused and perplexing. To resolve the mystery and to provide a guide to the perplexed, Muslim theologians have argued over the centuries that the second group must consult the teachings of Islam to regain their spiritual bearings. To put this serious Muslim theological point in humorous terms using an American electronic metaphor, one could say that Muslims are telling their religious cousins in the Abrahamic tradition that whenever they call up the telephone exchanges of the heavenly host, the angelic operators would repeat: "The number you have reached is not in service; please check the Holy Quran for the latest area code changes and additional messages."

The third category is made up of humans who remain outside the pale of believers, and are known to Muslim theologians as unbelievers (*kafirun*). Unwilling to accept the unseen as described by the Holy Prophet of Islam, and determined to lead a life of unbelief and corruption, these men and women are called many names by the Holy Quran. They are "deaf, blind and dumb"; they are the ones who willfully and consciously wrong their souls; they are confederates of Satan and are destined for the fires of hell. They can be atheistic or polytheistic. Their lives are empty and they are enamored with this life on Earth.

ISLAMIC PROSCRIPTIONS ABOUT THE TREATMENT OF THE OTHER

According to Islamic tradition, those who do not believe as Muslims do are treated according to the teachings of the Holy Quran and the examples of the Prophet. Christians and Jews, as stated above, are considered "People of the Book" (ahl al-kitab). Because of this classification, relations between these people and Muslims are theoretically harmonious. Muslims are supposed to treat them with respect as fellow beneficiaries of the Abrahamic heritage. There are several verses in the Quran which draw attention to the spiritual bonds that exist between the Muslim and the two predecessor faith communities that came into being as a result of the prophetic mission of the Prophet Moses and Jesus, the Messiah of the children of Israel. This understanding of relationships between Muslims and the ahl al-kitab (People of the Book) receives reinforcement in the hadith literature.

With respect to the unbelievers, the Holy Quran calls upon Muslims to spread the message of Islam among their fellow humans. They should apply rational arguments to explain the true reality of the Creator. However, while urging Muslims to employ all the rational arguments at their disposal, the Holy Quran commanded them to deal firmly with the people who are in a state of ignorance (jahiliyyah). Whenever these peoples of the age of ignorance create problems for Muslims in a given society, it is recommended that Muslims leave that abode and migrate (hijrah) to another territory where they can practice their faith with impunity. There are historical evidences to back up this claim.

During the Meccan days, when life was extremely difficult for the small community of Muslim believers, the Holy Prophet found it necessary for his Companions (sahaba) to take shelter in Abyssinia, on the Horn of Africa. Known as the "People of the Ship," these men and women who had sought refuge in Africa at the height of persecution, decided to return after the triumph of the Muslims in Arabia.

From this experience, Muslims have learned that, although migration (hijrah) is one alternative to living under oppressive and ignorant systems of government, they are not to accept aggression against themselves and their families. Whenever they are attacked by unbelievers, they should defend themselves accordingly. Hence the notion of jihad, a concept that has become one of the greatest sources of misunderstanding between Muslims and non-Muslims around the world. This idea of jihad is not meant to shed blood just for the sake of doing so. Actually there are two kinds of jihad. There is al-jihad al-akbar and al-jihad al-asghar. The first jihad is the great jihad whose objective is to subdue the satanic element within the human being. In other words, to wage this *jihad* successfully, the human being must master his appetites and passions. This is the only way he or she can differentiate himself or herself from the unbelievers. The second *jihad* is the *jihad* which addresses the challenge and threat to the stability and tranquility of the Muslim community (*ummah*). Those who pose threat to the community (*ummah*) must and should be resisted at all cost. Muslims are asked by their religion (*din*) to sacrifice for the common defense of the community. The *jihad* becomes the vehicle through which the integrity and continuity of the threatened community (*ummah*) is safeguarded. Indeed, the *jihad* becomes the last and final instrument by which the community (*ummah*) asserts and protects its territorial and communal imperative.

ISLAM AND THE NOTION OF "CHOSEN" OR "ELECTED" PEOPLE

In our attempt to dialog with Christians and Jews, it is important that we explain to them our understanding of certain concepts which are unfamiliar to the uninitiated among faith communities where these concepts and terms are alien. In the Muslim tradition, we do not speak of the "chosen" or "elected" people. Rather, we follow the statement which says that "God guides whomsoever He pleases." This statement has been interpreted by some Muslim scholars to mean that God opens the hearts of certain people to His message. When this message reaches them, they rush to the call. This notion of divine selection is not limited to one racial, ethnic or language group. There are no groups which can claim such divine favoritism for themselves alone. There is no preference with which the Creator gives the opportunity to serve Him. A person's rewards will depend on not who he is, but simply on what he has done to serve God. The Holy Quran states categorically that the best among human beings is the one who is most virtuous (*taqwa*). If there is a statement concerning human status in the peoples of God, which reverberates in the firmaments of Muslim thought, it can only be rivaled by the more prevalent and dominant *Allahu akbar* (Allah is Greater).

ISLAMIC TEACHINGS ON MISSIONARY WORK AND CONVERSION

In explaining the nature of missionary work to Christians and Jews, Muslims should make it categorically clear that the prophetic example of missionary work is the best. The Quran constantly reminded the Holy Prophet that he was a guide, that is, a messenger of the divine message, a bringer of glad tidings and a reminder to those who wish to forget the message of God. Given the fact that Muslims are supposed to follow the example of the Prophet Muhammad, it is therefore not surprising to see each and every Muslim propagator of the faith (*dai*) quote the same verses of the Holy Quran that God inspired the Holy Prophet to reveal to the people of Mecca and Medina.

In my reading of the Quran and the traditions of the Muslim community, I have come to the conclusion that missionary work directed toward the non-Muslims is part and parcel of the Islamic faith. Muslims are told by the Holy Quran that the word of God is not tampered with and its beauty should be brought to the attention of others in this life. To do missionary work, therefore, is to travel to the straight path (*sirat al-mustaqim*) and in doing so, lead others who might otherwise have strayed.

ISLAM AND THE PLURALISTIC SOCIAL UNIVERSE

In our attempt to shed light on Muslim opinions on and attitudes toward pluralism, it should be stated that pluralism is not strange to Muslims, whether they are the majority or minority community. From the Quranic and Hadith sources, we learn that whether in Mecca or in Medina, Muslims co-existed with non-Muslims. What needs to be pointed out here is that the Muslim understanding of pluralism is different from the dominant secular model which is described as "civil religion" by some and non-establishmentarianism by others. From an Islamic perspective, a society with different religious communities, such as Muslims, Christians and Jews, can co-exist under God so long as the Unity of God is not compromised. In a Muslim majority situation, the Muslim argues, non-Muslims are entitled to all the rights of self and community determination within the framework of Muslim majority rule. This is to say that non-Muslims living in a Muslim majority universe should have no illusion that they can ever change the Islamic paradigm through any human device which one could identify with social engineering. To put it another way, one could say that in a Muslim majority situation, Muslims believe that no material and historical transformations in human society could be revolutionary or earth shaking enough to bring about a change in the rule of Divine Principles as revealed in the Holy Quran and reinforced by the sayings of the Holy Prophet. This faith in the finality of the message of Islam is primary in shaping the Muslim attitude toward pluralism. Unwilling to trust the affairs of human governance exclusively to human devices and human reason, and firmly convinced that human life is for the express purpose of serving Allah, Muslims who are steadfast in their faith and are not apologetic about their beliefs would see pluralism differently from those who entrust governance to human beings who govern in accordance with rules and laws thought out by fellow humans. It is this differential approach to the metaphysical that separates Muslims from pluralists who are too secular to trust their lives to men acting on behalf of Heaven and too cynical to bank heavily on the goodwill of the majority community. Unlike those secularists who embrace the notion of civil religion to "protect" their minority communities within a society where their best safeguards are constitutional guarantees enshrined in a constitution, the Muslim advocate of the Islamic paradigm of pluralism would say that security for the minority can best be safeguarded if the spiritual commonwealth is united not by the secularism of the day but by the community of faith in a Supreme Being and by the common recognition of Adamite roots. Conversely, the Muslim minority in a non-Muslim majority situation would suffer the consequences of minority status so long as the majority community is not committed to ignorance or neo-ignorance. This type of community both undermines and compromises a Muslim's faith in Allah. The historical example of Muslims seeking refuge in Abyssinia makes it clear that life under the People of the Book is acceptable, although life in Darul Islam is most preferable.

THE NEGOTIABLE AND THE NON-NEGOTIABLE WITHIN THE ISLAMIC UNIVERSE

This final question needs to be treated with caution and diligence. Three things are negotiable in Muslim society. The first is that category of deeds and human actions which are classified by Muslim theologians as allowable (*halal*). In this area of action, Muslims should be able to deal with non-Muslims with little or no difficulty. Owing to these opportunities, Muslims should be able to bridge the social and cultural gaps between their communities and their non-Muslim neighbors as long as they engage in acts not proscribed as forbidden (*haram*).

The second thing that is negotiable is Muslim cooperation with others in the service of human kind. Christians and Jews in dialogue with Muslims must come to the realization that progress toward greater cooperation between the faith communities can only come about when

Muslims can feel secure with their cousins in the Abrahamic tradition and when the religious cousins can feel likewise. The final item that is negotiable in Islam is cooperation with the People of the Book in the field of knowledge other than religious knowledge. Those who wish to further the cause of dialogue must appreciate the Muslim thirst for knowledge, if and when they have the sophistication and the historical awareness of what the Islamic religion contributed to the pool of human knowledge in the ancient world. There are Quranic and Hadith injunctions urging Muslims to gather as much knowledge as possible. Almost every Muslim child from a sophisticated Muslim home knows the story of the Holy Prophet telling his followers to seek knowledge as distant as China.

The list of non-negotiable rules includes the following:

1. There will never be Muslim compromise on the unity of God (*tawhid*).

2. Muslims who know their faith well, and are committed to its defense, will never compromise on the finality of the revelation given to Prophet Muhammad.

3. Muslims will never accept the doctrine of original sin.

4. Muslims will never be swayed by rationalistic and "scientific" arguments to question the purified character of Mary, Mother of Jesus.

5. Muslims will never accept the arguments of those who question the Virgin Birth of Jesus.

6. Muslims will never accept the idea that Jesus died for our human sins.

7. Muslims will never accept the doctrine of redemption and atonement.

8. Muslims will never abandon their belief in the unseen.

9. Muslims will never negotiate whether there is a life beyond the grave.

10. Muslims will never negotiate about the possibility of heaven or hell.

In Summary

Hopefully, the material presented above will serve as the basis for future dialogue between Muslims and non-Muslims from the Abrahamic traditions. We must always remember that we live on a planet that is shrinking daily because of our own accomplishments as creatures of God the Creator. Unless and until we learn to speak to each other in a language that reflects our common roots in Adam, this dialogue is impossible. We must recognize that, here on earth, we are truly the carpenters and masons charged with the task of building not another Tower of Babel, but a Kabah of human responsibility, a church of human love and a temple of justice among men, women and children on this planet.

11

THE DARUL ISLAM MOVEMENT: NOTES ON AN UNDERSTUDIED SUNNI ISLAMIC MOVEMENT

The Darul Islam Movement, later known as the Ya-Sin Mosque, was a concept first born in 1962 by three brothers: Rajab Muhammad, Ishaq Abdush Shahead and Abdul Kareem. According to the *al-Jihadul Akbar*, they "had as their primary objective the establishment of an organic, functioning Islamic Community."[1] Originally they were associated with the late Shakyh Daud Faisal and his Islamic Mission of America (IMA) and they attended Friday prayer at the IMA Center at State Street in Brooklyn, New York.

However, as the Darul Islam Movement developed, the three founders "grew dissatisfied with the directional focus of the Islamic Mission, whose leadership came exclusively from the Middle East and who were either unaware of or unresponsive to the needs of the indigenous people in whose midst they had settled."[2] In fact, many early African-American converts to Islam, sharing facilities with the immigrant Muslims, harbored this sentiment of neglect. This happened in Chicago where Dr. Mufti Sadiq and Sufi Bengalie of the Ahmadiyya movement preached to Afro-Americans in the 1920s and 1930s. In fact, some have alleged that the followers of Marcus Garvey, who gravitated towards Islam, at first moved to the Ahmadiyya Movement but later branched out because of the same feelings expressed above by the founding fathers of the Darul Islam Movement.

This common feeling of disregard by immigrant Muslims toward African-Americans who had recently converted to Islam stems from three important factors—the racial climate between the two Islamic fac-

143

tions, the opinion that members of the MSA were transient and lacking the ability to propagate Islam in America and the overall resentment of foreign ideas embedded in American psychology.

The first factor leading to this conflict was the racial climate emanating from foreign Muslims operating amongst African-Americans. Most of these immigrants were invariably South Asian and Middle Easterners who generally perceive themselves either as "whites" or "browns." This racial self-identification of the foreign Muslim was very important to the Afro-American Muslim who saw himself as a social being forced to live by the norms of the American society. As a response to a workshop at the 12th Annual MSA Convention at the University of Toledo, Ohio (August 30-September 1974), the *Jihadul Akbar* reinforced the African-American sentiment that there was a lack of indigenous American involvement in the decision-making process of the Muslim Student Association (MSA). It wrote:

> The point was made that "foreign" Muslims were accepting the racial conditions imposed upon them by non-Muslim Americans and Canadians. The American verbal tirade suggested that the future of Islam was threatened if there were a continued exclusion of American Muslims from decision making and problem solving. This session came to an abrupt halt wherein the members of African-American descent called for their own "caucus" or strategy meeting.[3]

It was not only the racial tensions between the Muslim immigrants and the African-American converts that led the latter group to feel neglected in their path to spiritual knowledge. There was also a feeling that the students and professionals in the Muslim Student Association were transient, disrupting the propagation of Islam necessary in order for it to develop properly in America. In an article assessing the future of Islam in America, the *al-Jihadul Akbar* pointed out that there existed African-American Muslims who strongly believed that foreign-born Muslims should leave the task of planting, cultivating and nurturing the budding Islam to their American brothers.

> The M.S.A. has a lot of good brothers but a few have personal ambitions. It's the ambitious ones who want to direct Islamic affairs in this country. They are not from this country.

Americans should control our own activity and they should "assist" us.[4]

This continuing phenomenon of native American resentment toward foreign promoters of Islam ultimately can be traced to American social-psychology itself. The inherent suspicion of foreign ideas is very familiar to students of American society, and in this context one can suggest that American nativism is color-blind and transethnic in America. Owing to the reality of this fact, one can acknowledge that the resentment of foreign control of Islamic organizations, due to the afore-mentioned reasons propelled enterprising and seriously committed American Muslims to found organizations of their own, which catered to their own needs and desires.

It is indeed against this background that we examine the Darul Islam Movement and the decision of the founding fathers to break away from Shaykh Daud Faisal's Islamic Mission of America, which they believed was heavily dominated by foreign Muslims. To achieve their objectives, these African-American Muslim leaders set out in 1962 to mobilize new members from amongst the "poor and downtrodden of New York slums and ghettoes" and by 1963, Rajab Mahmud was elect-ed as the first Imam of the Darul Islam Movement, and distinct progress was made in building the organization.

Gradually the Darul Islam Movement established itself and found-ed its first headquarters at 1964 Atlantic Avenue in Brooklyn. Later the organization was moved to new quarters at Downing Street but due to the enrollment of 150 new members and the increases in attendance to the daily prescribed prayers, the organization was later moved to new and larger quarters at Downing Street. But in the meantime, the move-ment's unsettled nature caused it to, "at various times [meet] in apart-ments, in storefront, and in lofts before settling at Saratoga Avenue in 1965."[5]

Not only was its physical size expanding, but the Darul Islam Movement began to extend its sphere of influence by linking up with other Muslim communities across the U .S. Within the first six years of its existence the Movement had established branches along the eastern seaboard, in the south and in the midwest.

According to their news organ, the *al-Jihadul Akbar*, at the MSA east coast meeting in the spring of 1969 in Pawling, New York, Muslims from various communities discussed, "the need for national unity among U. S. born citizens of the faith."[6] The following organizations were represented at the meeting: al-Ansar al-Islam (Amir Hassan), Community Mosque (Yusuf M. Hamid), Afro-American Ummat (Abu Bakr), International Muslim Brotherhood (Nafi Muhaimin).

The efforts toward unity made at the conference in Pawley, New York did not materialize and the native Muslims remained just as divided as before. Things however changed for the better in 1973, when a group of Arabs interested in local American unity arranged a meeting for all the groups interested in the creation of one national Islamic organization. According to Hajj Muhammad, a writer of the *al-Jihadul Akbar*, this effort succeeded perhaps because "the setting of the meeting this time being in Mecca and Medina for the promise of financial support changed the hearts of many brothers."[7] Various community organizations convened for this meeting and as a result a new umbrella organization came into being. Known as the Council of Islamic Organizations, this new organization allowed each of its member units to keep their individual title and identity. However, due to a disagreement with the other organizations and with policy for this new organization, the Darul Islam Movement decided to pull out.

During this period of isolation, the Darul Islam Movement encountered serious difficulties with the law and with rival Muslim groups in the black community. One year after its break with the Council of Islamic Organizations "two Ministers from Darul Islam were mysteriously shot to death while in their house of worship, Ya-Sin Mosque in Brooklyn."[8]

In 1974, at an MSA convention in Toledo, Ohio, a group of North American Muslims met on the lawn outside of the convention hall to lay down plans for a national organization of native-born American Muslims. The Darul Islam Movement attended this session and agreed with the planners that a conference specifically for North American Muslim Communities be held so that they could discuss and plan moves for unity. A meeting was held in Chicago, but because its proceedings and resolutions were not made available to the Darul Islam Movement, its leaders decided to withdraw. In retrospect, one can now argue that the Movement was subjected to tremendous pressure at this time. The killings of some of the founders of the movement and the frequency with which its leaders came into contact with the law enforcement agencies made the future of the group less and less secure.

Since 1974 the Darul Islam has lost its momentum, although its constructive elements are still around in their respective cities in America. The Darul Islam's idea of a national organization for all Sunni is still to be realized, and though its teachings differ from Darul Islam, the American Muslim Mission comes close to such a continental body. Whereas leaders of the Darul Islam Movement such as Bilal Abdul Rahman (one of the two men slain at the mosque in Brooklyn, New York), talked of creating their own Islamic army and wage *jihad*, the American Muslim Mission is concerned about teaching its followers to accept America as their homeland and to act on the teachings of Islam so as to transform her morally and spiritually through example and hardwork.

NOTES TO 11
THE DARUL ISLAM MOVEMENT: NOTES ON AN
ʿUNDERSTUDIED SUNNI ISLAMIC MOVEMENT

1 See *al-Jihadul Akbar*, Vol. 1 No. 1 p.

2 *Ibid.*

3 *Ibid*, p.7.

4 *Al-Jihadul Akbar*, November, 1974, p.7.

5 See Hajj Muhammad, "Darul Islam in Isolation," *al-Jihadul Akbar*, Vol.1 No.1.

6 *Al-Jihadul Akbar*, Vol.1 No.3, p.7.

7 *Ibid.*

8 *Ibid.*

Select Bibliography

Abraham, Sameer Y; and Abraham, Nabeel, ed. *Arabs in the New World*. Detroit, Michigan: Wayne State University Press, 1983.

Alford, Terry. *Prince Among Slaves. The Story of an African Prince Sold in the American South*. New York: Oxford University Press, 1977.

Abu-Rabi, Ibrahim M. *Intellectual Origins of Islamic Resurgence in the Modern Arab World* .

Abu Saud, Mahmoud and Gad-Harf, David. *Bridging the Faiths. An Agenda for Jewish Community Relations* . Washington, D.C.: American Muslim Council, 1993; Albany: State University of New York Press, 1996.

Ahmad, Akbar S. and Donnan, Hastings ed. *Islam, Globalization and Post Modernity*. New York: Routledge, 1994.

al-Faruqi, Ismail. *Tawhid: Its Implications for Thought and Life*. Herndon, Virginia: International Institute of Islamic Thought, 1982.

_____, *The Islamization of Knowledge: General Principles and Workplan*. Washington, D.C.: International Institute of Islamic Thought, 1982.

Ali, Abdullah Yusuf. *The Holy Quran-Text, Translation, Commentary*. Indianapolis: MSA, 1975.

Ali, Kamal. "Islamic Education in the United States: An Overview of Issues, Problems and Possible Approaches," *The American Journal of Islamic Social Sciences*, 1984, pp.127-132.

Alkali, Nura, Adamu, Adamu, Yadudu, Awwal, Motem, Rashid, Salihi, Haruna. *Islam in Africa*. Proceedings of the Islam in Africa Conference Lagos: Spectrum Books, 1993.

Aswad, Barbara ed. *Arab-Speaking Communities in American Cities* Staten Island, New York: Center for Migration Studies, 1974.

Austin, Allan D. *African Muslims in Antebellum America: A Sourcebook.* New York: Garland Publishing Company, 1995.

Austin, Allan D. *African Muslims in Antebellum America: Transatlantic Stories and Spiritual Struggles.* New York: Routledge, 1997.

Bagby, Ihsan "Is ISNA an Islamic Movement?" *Islamic Horizons,* March 1986, p.4.

Barboza, Steven. *American Jihad: Islam after Malcolm X.* New York: Doubleday, 1994.

Bargai, Leona. *The East Indians and the Pakistanis.* Minneapolis, Minnesota: Lerner Publications, 1967.

Barzangi, Nimat Hafez. "The Education of North American Muslim Parents and Children: Conceptual Change as a Contribution to Islamization of Education," *The American Journal of Islamic Social Sciences,* Vol. 7, No. 3 (December, 1990), pp. 385-402.

Ba-Yunus, Ilyas. *Muslims in North America: Problems and Prospects.* Plainfield, Indiana: Muslim Student Association, 1974.

Beyer, Peter. *Religion and Globalization.* London: Sage Publications, 1994.

Bousquet, G. H. "Moslem Religious Influences in the United States," *Moslem World* 25 (1935).

Braden, Charles S. "Islam in America," *International Review of Mission* 48 (July 1959).

Braibanti, Ralph. *The Nature and Structure of the Islamic World.* Chicago: International Strategy and Policy Institute, 1995.

Bretton-Granator, Gary, Weiss, Andrea. *Shalom/Salaam: A Resource for Jewish/Muslim.* Dialogue New York: United American Hebrew Congregations Press, 1993.

Cogley, John ed. *Religion in America: Original Essays on Religion in a Free Society.* New York: Meridian Books, Inc., 1958.

Crane, Robert D "Civilization in Crisis: Confrontation or Peaceful Engagement," *The American Muslim* Vol. 2, No. 9 (Winter, 1994).

Curtin, Phillip D. ed.*Narratives by West Africans from the Era of the Slave Trade.* Madison, Wisconsin: The University of Wisconsin Press, 1967.

Davidson, Basil. *Lost Cities of Africa.* Boston: Little Brown, 1959.

_____, *The African Past.* New York: Grosset & Dunlap, 1964

_____, *African Civilization Revisited.* Trenton, New Jersey: Africa

World Press, 1991.

El-Amin, Mustafa. *The Religion of Islam and the Nation of Islam: What is the Difference*. Newark, New Jersey: El-Amin Production, 1991.

El-Kholy, Abdo. *The Arab Moslems in the United States: Religion and Assimilation*. New Haven, Connecticut: College and University Press, 1983.

Fluehr-Lobban, Carolyn. *Islamic Society in Practice*.   Gainesville, Florida: University Press of Florida, 1994.

Esposito, John L. *Islam The Straight Path*. New York: Oxford University Press, 1988.

_____, *The Islamic Threat Myth or Reality*. New York: Oxford University Press, 1992.

Essien-Udom, Essien Udosen. *Black Nationalism: A Search for Identity in America*. Chicago: The University of Chicago Press, 1962.

Fage, J. D. *A History of Africa*. New York: Routledge, 1988.

Farrakhan, Louis. *A Torchlight for Islam*. Philadelphia: P.C. International, 1989.

Freye, Gilberto. *The Masters and the Slaves*. New York: Alfred Knopf, 1946.

Gilles, Kel. *Allah in the West: Islamic Movements in America and Europe*. Stanford: Stanford University Press, 1997.

Ghanea-Bassiri, Kambiz. *Competing Visions of Islam in the United States: A Study of Los Angeles Westport*. Connecticut: Greenwood Press, 1997.

Grose, George B.; Hubbard, Benjamin B. eds. *The Arabian Connections: A Jew, Christian and Muslim in Dialogue* . Notre Dame, Indiana: Published by the Africa World Press and the Academy for Judaic, Christian,and Islamic Studies, 1994.

Haddad, Yvonne Z; Haines, Byron; and Findley, Ellison. eds. *The Islamic Impact*. Syracuse: Syracuse University Press, 1984.

Haddad, Yvonne Z. ed. *The Muslims of America*. Oxford University, 1991.

Haddad, Yvonne Z; Haddad, Wadi ed. *Christian-Muslim Encounters*. Gainesville, Florida: University Press of Florida, 1995.

Haddad, Yvonne Z. and Jane Idleman Smith eds. *Muslim Communities in the United States*. Albany: State University of New York Press, 1994.

Haddad, Yvonne and Jane Idleman Smith ed. *Mission to America.* Gainesville, Florida: University Press of Florida, 1993.

Haddad, Yvonne Z.; Lummis, Adair T. *Islamic Values in the United States: A Comparative Study.* New York: Oxford University Press, 1987.

Haines, Byron; and Cooley, Frank L. ed. Christians and Muslims Together: An Exploration by Presbyterians. Philadelphia: Geneva Press, 1987.

Hirst, Paul; and Hirst, Graham ed. *Globalization in Question.* Oxford: Oxford University Press, 1996.

Hussain, Asad; Woods, John; and Akhter, Javed. ed. *Muslims in America. Opportunities and Challenges.* Chicago, Illinois: International Strategy and Policy Institute, 1996.

Husaini, Zohra. *Muslims in the Canadian Mosaic.* Edmonton, Alberta, Canada: Muslim Research Foundation, 1990.

Idries, Jafar. "Is Man the Viceregent of God." *Journal of Islamic Studies* (Oxford), January 1990.

Irving, T.B. *The Quran.* Brattleboro, Vermont: Amana Books, 1985.

_____, "King Zumbi and the Male Movement in Brazil," *The American Journal of Islamic Social Sciences,* Volume 9, Number 3 (Fall, 1992), pp. 397-409.

Johnson, Steve "Political Activity of Muslims in America," in Yvonne Z. Haddad, ed. *The Muslims of America.* New York: Oxford University Press, 1991.

Kaplan, Sidney. *The Black Presence in the Era of the American Revolution 1770-1800.* New York: New York Graphic Society Ltd. and Smithsonian Institution Press, 1973.

Khalidi, Omar. *Indian Muslims in North America.* Watertown, Mass: South Asia Press, 1989.

Kinney, Jay. "Sufism comes to America," *Gnosis,* Number 30, Winter 94.

Khan, Lurey. "An American Pursues Her Pakistani Past," *Asia* (a publication of The Asia Society) March/April, 1980, pp. 34-39.

Khan, Salim. "Pakistanis in the Western United States," *Journal of Institute of Muslim Minority Affairs,* Vol.5, No.1 (1983-84), pp.36-46.

Levinson, David; and Ember, Melvin, ed. *American Immigrant Cultures. Builders of a Nation.* New York: Simon and Schuster Macmillan, 1997.

Lincoln, C. Eric. *The Black Muslims in America*. 3rd. ed. Trenton, New Jersey: Africa World Press, 1994

_____, *Race, Religion and the Continuing American Dilemma*. New York: Hill & Wang, 1984.

_____, *My Face Is Black*. Boston: Beacon, 1964.

_____, *The American Muslim Mission in the Context of American Social History in the Muslim Community in North America*, edited by Earl H. Waugh, Baha Abu-Laban, and Regula B. Qureshi. Edmonton, Alberta: University of Alberta Press, 1983.

_____, ed. *The Black Experience in Religion*. Garden City, New York: Anchor Books, 1974.

Lomax, Louis. *When the Word is Given: A Report on Elijah Muhammad, Malcolm X, and the Black Muslim World*. Westport, Connecticut: Greenwood, 1963.

Makdisi, Nadim. "The Moslems of America," *The Christian Century*, 26 August 1959.

Malik, Salahuddin. "Pakistanis," in David Levinson and Melvin Ember, ed. *American Immigrant: Cultures Builders of a Nation*. New York: Simon and Schuster: Macmillan, 1997.

Mamiya, Lawrence H. "From Black Muslim to Bilalian: The Evolution of a Movement," *Journal for the Scientific Study of Religion*, Vol. 21, No. 2 (June 1992), pp.138-52.

Marsh, Clifton E. *From Black Muslims to Muslims: The Transition from Separation to Islam*, 1930-1980. Metuchen, New Jersey: Scarecrow Press, 1984.

Maududi, Syed A.A. *Towards Understanding Islam*. Plainfield, Indiana: The ISNA Islamic Book Service, 1977.

Mazrui, Ali A. "Global Africa in Flux: The Dialectic of Diversity in the Black World," in Carlos Moore et al., *African Presence in the Americas*. Trenton, New Jersey: Africa World Press, 1995, pp. 357-76.

_____, "Between the Crescent and the Star-spangled Banner: American Muslims in U.S. Foreign Policy," *International Affairs* (London).

McCloud, Aminah. *African-American Islam*. New York: Routledge, 1995.

Millman, Joel. *The Other Americans: How Immigrants Renew Our*

Country, Our Economy and Our Values. New York: Viking Press, 1997.

Miller, Randall M, and Marzik, Thomas D. *Immigrants and Religion in Urban America*. Philadelphia: Temple University Press, 1977.

Mittleman, James H. ed. Globalization: *Critical Reflections*. Boulder, Colorado: Lynne Rienner, 1996.

Mohammed, Warith Deen. *Focus on Al-Islam*. Chicago: Zakat, 1988.

_____, *An African-American Genesis*. Chicago: Progressions, 1986.

_____, *Al-Islam, Unity and Leadership*. Chicago: Sense Maker, 1991.

Moore, Carlos; Sanders, Tanya R.; and Moore, Shawna ed. *African Presence in the Americas*. Trenton, New Jersey: Africa World Press, Inc., 1995.

Moore, Kathleen. "New Claimants to Religious Tolerance and Protection: A Case Study of American and Canadian Muslims." *The American Journal of Islamic Social Sciences*, Volume 6, Number 1 (September 1989), pp.135-42.

Moore, Wilbert E. "Global Sociology: The World as a Single System," *American Journal of Sociology*, Vol. 71 (1996), pp.475-482.

Muhammad, Elijah. *Message to the Blackman in America*. Chicago: Muhammad Mosque of Islam No. 2, 1965.

_____, *The Theology of Time*. Newport News, Virginia: UBUS Graphics and Printing, 1992.

Murata, Sachiko and Chittick, William C. *The Vision of Islam*. New York: Paragon House, 1994.

Naff, Alixa. *Becoming American: The Early Arab Immigrant Experience*. Carbondale and Edwardsville, Illinois: Southern Illinois University Press, 1985.

Nasr, Seyyed Hossein. *A Young Muslim's Guide to the Modern World*. Chicago: KAZI Publications, 1993.

_____, *Man and Nature: The Spiritual Crisis of Modern Man*. London: Unwin Paperbacks, 1976.

_____, *Islam and the Plight of Modern Man*. London: Longman Group Ltd., 1975.

_____, "To Live in a World With No Center-and Many," *Cross Currents*, Volume 46, Number 3, Fall 1996, pp. 318-325.

_____, *Traditional Islam in the Modern World*. London/New York: Kegan Paul International, 1987.

Numan, Fareed H. *The Muslim Population in the United States: A Brief Statement*. Washington, D.C.: American Muslim Council, 1992.

Nyang, Sulayman S. "Islam in the United States of America: A Review of the Sources." *Islamic Culture*, April1981, pp. 91-109.

_____, "The Stuff That Dreams Are Made Of." *Arabia: The Islamic World Review*, November 1982, p. 24.

Nyang, Sulayman; and Ahmad, Mumtaz. "The Muslim Intellectual Emigre in the United States." *Islamic Culture*, July 1985.

_____, "A New Beginning for the Black Muslims," *Arabia: The Islamic World Review*, (July, 1985), pp. 50-51.

Nyang, S. "Islam in North America," in Stewart Sutherland et al., *The World's Religions*. London:

Poston, Larry. *Islamic Dawah in the West: Muslim Missionary Activity and the Dynamics of Conversion to Islam*. New York: Oxford University Press, 1992.

Prpic, George J. South. *Slavic Immigration in America*. Boston: Twayne Publishers, 1977.

Quick, Abdullah Hakim. *Deeper Roots Muslims in the Americas and the Caribbean From Before Columbus to the Present*. London: Taha Publishers, 1996.

Rahman, Fazlur. *Islam*. Chicago: University of Chicago Press, 1966

_____, *Major Themes of the Quran*. Chicago: Bibliotheca Islamica, 1980.

_____, *Islam and Modernity*. Chicago: The University of Chicago Press, 1982.

Robbins, Thomas; and Robertson, Roland ed. *Church-State Relations: Tensions and Transitions*. New Brunswick, New Jersey: Transactions Books, 1997.

Said, Edward. *Covering Islam*. London: Routledge and Kegan Paul, 1981.

Sakr, Ahmad. *Islam and Muslims*. Hiawatha, Iowa: Cedar Graphics, Inc. 1994.

Sarna, Jonathan D. "The American Jewish Experience and the Emergence of the Muslim Community in America." *The American Journal of Islamic Social Sciences*, Vol. 9, No. 3 (1989).

Shafiq, Muhammad. *The Growth of Islamic Thought in North America: Focus on Ismail Raji al-Faruqi.* Brentwood, Maryland: Amana Publications, 1994.

Shaheen, Jack G. *The TV Arab.* Colorado: Popular Press, 1984

_____, *"Abscam: Arabophobia in America."* ADC Issues, Vol. 1, 1988.

Siddiqui, Muzamil H. "Muslims in Non-Muslim Society." *Islamic Horizons,* May /June 1986.

Sonn, Tamara. *Islam and the Question of Minorities.* Atlanta: Scholars Press, 1996.

Speight, Marston. "Christian-Muslim Dialogue in the United States of America." *Islamochristiana,* Vol. 7 (1981), pp.201-210.

Stankievich, Joan. *The White Ruthenian Mohammedans of Brooklyn.* (a publication published by author in 1953).

Suleiman, Michael W. "Arab-Americans: A Community Profile," *Journal Institute of Muslim Minority Affairs,* Vol.5, No.1 (1983-84), pp. 29-35.

_____, "America and the Arabs: Negative Images and the Feasibility of Dialogue." *Arab Studies Quarterly,* Vol. 11, No. 213.

Trimmingham, J. Spencer. *Sufi Orders.* London: Oxford University, 1971.

Tunison, Emory H. "Mohammed Alexander Russell Webb: First American Muslim." *The Arab World,* Vol.1, No.3 (1945): pp. 13-18.

Turner, Richard Brent. *Islam in the African-American Experience.* Bloomington, Indiana: Indiana University Press, 1997.

_____, "The Ahmadiyya Mission to Blacks in the United States in the 1920's. " *Journal of Religious Thought,* Vol. 44 (Spring, 1988), pp. 50-66.

_____, "The Ahmadiyya Movement in America." *Religion Today* (England), Volume 5, Number 3 (1990)

Van Sertima, Ivan. *They Came Before Columbus.* New York: Random House, 1976.

_____, *African Presence in Early America.* New Brunswick, New Jersey: Transaction Publishers, 1995.

Waldman, Marilyn Robinson. *Muslims and Christians, Muslims and Jews: A Common Past, A Hopeful Future.* Columbus, Ohio: The

Islamic Foundation of Central Ohio, The Catholic Diocese of Columbus, and the Congregation Tifereth Israel, 1992.

Waugh, Earle; Abu-Laban, Baha; and Qureshi, Regina ed. *Muslim Community in North America*. Edmonton, Canada: University of Alberta Press, 1983.

Wiener, Leo. *Africa and the Discovery of America*. Philadelphia: Innes and Sons, 1922.

Winters, Clyde-Ahmad. "Afro-American Muslims: From Slavery to Freedom." *Islamic Studies*, Vol. 17, No. 4 (Winter 1978), pp.187-203.

_____, "Origins of Muslim Slaves in the U.S." *Al-itti-had*, 21 (September 1986), pp.49-51.

Wright, Jr., J. W. *Discrimination, Immigration, and the Economics of Being Arab and Believing in Islam in America*. (An unpublished Ph.D thesis submitted at Loughborough University, Loughborough, England).